SWEET · TO · WANDER
THROUGH · THIS · ENGLISH · LAND,
BY · MEAD · & · ORCHARD, COPSE
AND · OLD-WORLD · GRANGE,
LULLED · BY · THE · SONG
OF · BROOK · AND · BIRD · AND · BEE.

ALFRED HAYES

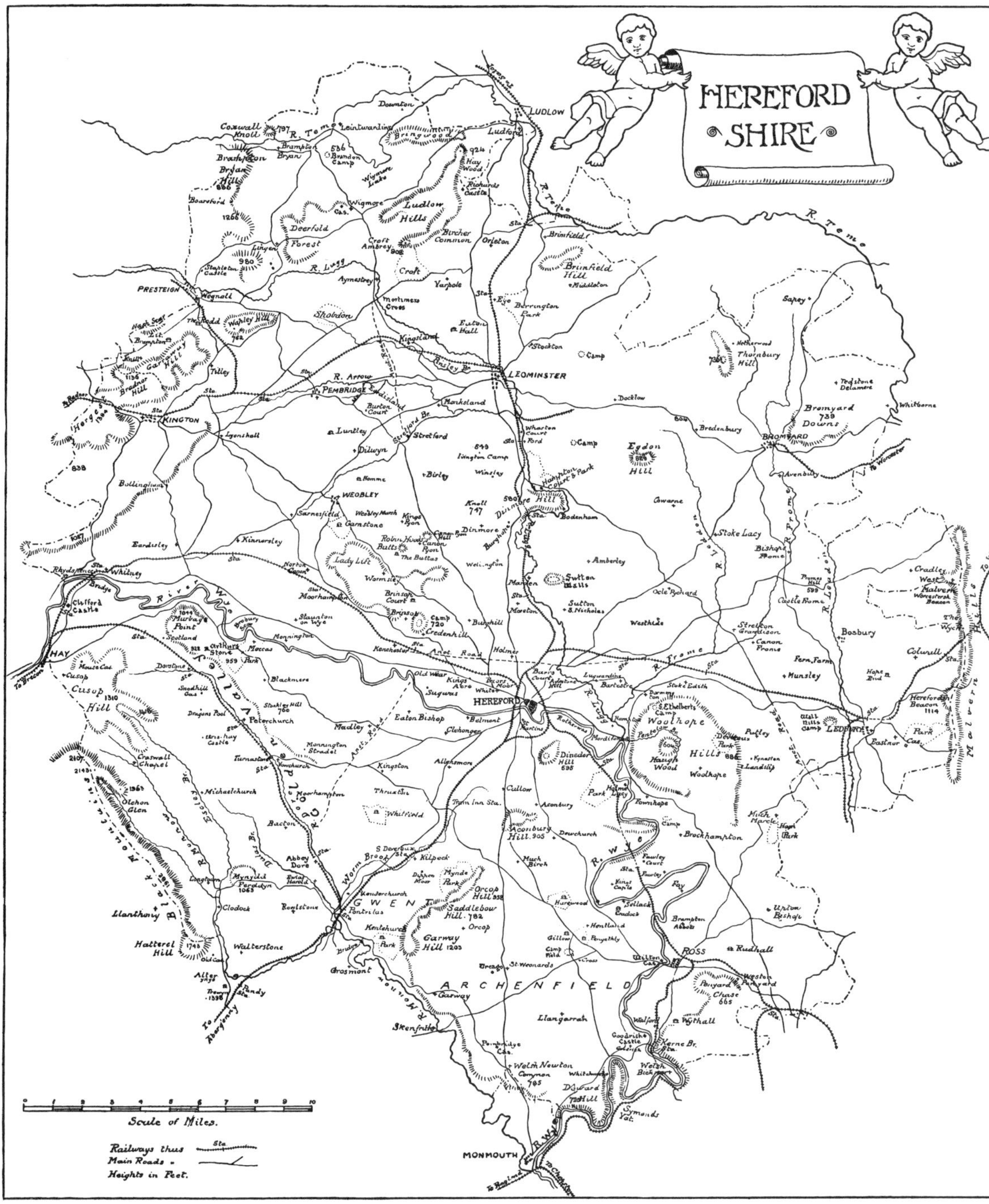
HEREFORD SHIRE
HEREFORD
LEOMINSTER
LUDLOW
KINGTON
PRESTEIGN
PEMBRIDGE
WEOBLEY
BROMYARD
LEDBURY
ROSS
HAY
MONMOUTH
ARCHENFIELD
Scale of Miles
Railways thus
Main Roads
Heights in Feet.

NOOKS AND CORNERS OF HEREFORDSHIRE.

Nooks and Corners
of
Herefordshire.

BY

H. THORNHILL TIMMINS.

WITH NUMEROUS ILLUSTRATIONS BY THE AUTHOR.

LONDON:
ELLIOT STOCK, 62, PATERNOSTER ROW, E.C.
1892.

Originally published in 1892
by Elliot Stock, London

Reprinted 1974

ISBN 0 9518589 1 2

Printed and bound by
SMITH SETTLE
Ilkley Road, Otley, West Yorkshire
for
Lapridge Publications
25 Church Street
Hereford HR1 2LR
Telephone (0432) 353586

INTRODUCTION

This year of re-publication of *Nooks and Corners of Herefordshire* marks the centenary of its first appearance. Originally published in London by Elliot Stock in 1892 it has always been a firm favourite amongst collectors. The first edition was handsomely produced in decorated cloth with pleasantly antique lettering and a gold blocked inset of the gatehouse at Brockhampton Court. Fifty special copies were printed on large paper and numbered. Evidence of the book's popularity is that copies of the original are usually found in fairly worn condition. Even so, half way decent copies fetch quite a lot of money nowadays.

Nooks and Corners of Herefordshire was published by subscription. This was a popular method of publishing books for which the publisher was unsure of the demand. A prospectus announcing the intention to publish was distributed amongst likely buyers who were invited to register their interest in a copy or copies prior to publication. If sufficient subscribers were obtained the publication could go ahead; those who had showed their faith in the book had the satisfaction of finding their names listed for all to see in the list of subscribers. When *Nooks and Corners* was reprinted in the 1970s the list of subscribers was omitted. It has been restored to this edition as it is of interest to local historians and bibliographers. An interesting sidelight is that one of the original subscribers, the Revd E. Palin of Linton near Ross-on-Wye, was the great grandfather of Michael Palin, the actor and writer, who based his film 'American Friends' on the life of his forebear.

The author and illustrator of *Nooks and Corners*, Henry Thornhill Timmins, was a Birmingham man who had trained as an architect but gave up that profession to 'follow his strong bent for art'. His father Frederick Timmins (no doubt the F. H. Timmins of Edgbaston in the list of subscribers) was a collector of what were known at the turn of the century as 'modern' watercolours, meaning David Cox and the like, and it is evident that the young Henry imbibed his love of art from an early age. Timmins and his wife travelled widely in England and abroad, extending their journeying to Egypt, India, Burma, and Ceylon. Lengthy visits to Italy and other countries of the south seem to have been frequent. There is not much evidence for Timmins's commercial activity as an artist although he was a contributor to the 'English Illustrated Magazine'. The frequency of his travels indicates that he was probably financially independent.

It is evident that *Nooks and Corners of Herefordshire*, Timmins's first book, was successful since it heralded a mini series of three titles. Herefordshire was followed in 1895 by *Nooks and Corners of Pembrokeshire* and in 1899 *Nooks and Corners of Shropshire* appeared. All were published in London by Elliot Stock in a similar format. Timmins does not appear to have published anything else. He died at Rome in 1908.

When Timmins travelled through Herefordshire in the summer of 1891 sketching and researching for this book he was a stranger to the county. He was in contact at that time with the ubiquitous Walter Pilley, local businessman, mayor of Hereford, and, above all, indefatigable collector of Herefordiana whose truly extensive collection resides now in Hereford Library. Some letters Timmins wrote to Pilley are preserved in Pilley's large paper copy of *Nooks and Corners*. Timmins wrote to Pilley from Weobley, where he and his wife were staying with 'Miss Pugh', asking for information about Brinsop which he had just visited and about which his interest had been roused. After his tour 'in beautiful Herefordshire' was finished he wrote again to Pilley from Harborne requesting information about 'the north-west quarter toward Wigmore, Presteigne and Knighton' naming eight or ten places he had seen including The Rodd 'of which I cannot as yet obtain any information; so I venture to ask if you can kindly help me, as you have done before'.

Pilley obliged and Timmins wrote in September from Hampstead (he was soon sailing for Naples en route to Sicily) to thank him for 'the detailed accounts of the places I mentioned – they are delightfully clear & systematic, and I shall be very glad to make use of them'. Make use of them he no doubt did although he does not make any acknowledgement to Pilley in the book. Timmins was essentially an artist and the book was a vehicle for his drawings. If he could get someone else to provide the facts he was more than happy to let them.

The abiding pleasure of *Nooks and Corners of Herefordshire* lies in Timmins's very pleasing line drawings. When the artist wrote of 'the romantic and beautiful scenery, for which this rural English county is so justly admired' one feels he wrote from the heart for he has so truly caught the spirit of Herefordshire a hundred years ago in the charming illustrations to this book. Here is Herefordshire in that nostalgic era when Victoria reigned. Although country life could be hard, it was relatively uncomplicated. This county was a lovely rural backwater with Hereford city 'environed on every hand by gardens and corn fields, hop-grounds and orchards'. Many indeed were the nooks and corners then to be found across the length and breadth of the county. Railway lines radiated from Hereford to carry the traveller in whichever direction he chose. Timmins could, for example, take a train first thing in the morning to Leominster and change to a branch line to continue his journey to Kingsland station where he got down and took a short cut by a field path to the village.

Of course, he did not always take the train. Sometimes he walked out of the city into the surrounding countryside on his way to, say, Weobley, by deserted lanes with their shady hedgerows 'garlanded with wild roses, and sweet with sinuous honeysuckle', and this within a stone's throw of the White Cross. Timmins lingered at Weobley. Like many a traveller before and since he was greatly taken with that lovely village for he found much to sketch there. All in all *Nooks and Corners of Herefordshire* contains some of the most memorable drawings of our county and the publishers are pleased to make them available once again, this time to a new generation of Herefordians a hundred years after the original publication.

The first edition of this book was favoured with a preface by the Revd Canon H. W. Phillott, then chancellor of Hereford Cathedral. As it has little relevance to today's reader it has been omitted from this edition. Otherwise, with the exception of this new introduction, the book is as it first appeared.

Paul Latcham

CONTENTS.

INDEX TO ILLUSTRATIONS.

NOOKS AND CORNERS OF HEREFORDSHIRE.

'Green the land is where my daily
  Steps in jocund childhood played ;
Dimpled close with hill and valley,
  Dappled very close with shade ;
Summer snow of apple-blossom
  Running up from glade to glade.'

ELIZABETH BARRETT BROWNING.

A GENERAL SURVEY. THE CITY OF HEREFORD.

HEREFORDSHIRE may be described as lying in a roughly circular plain, sheltered by the encompassing heights of the Malvern Hills on the one hand, and on the opposite or western boundary by the steep escarpments of the Black Mountains, buttressing for many a mile the highlands of wild Wales. Southwards the county abuts upon the hilly and wooded district of the Forest of Dean, through which the Wye breaks its way to the sea by the rugged gorge of Symonds Yat.

The district thus comprised forms the sunny and sheltered valley of the Wye, and its affluent streams of Lugg and Monnow ; while in the northern portion the river Teme tumbles along amidst picturesque scenery, entering the county beneath the wooded height of Coxwall Knoll, scene of the last struggle of the immortal Carâdoc ; and passing thence to Ludford, beneath an ancient bridge giving access to Ludlow and Shropshire.

The river Lugg is joined near Leominster by the Arrow, Pinsley, and other considerable streams watering the rich country around Pembridge and Weobley, while away to the south-west, where the foothills of the Black Mountains radiate not unlike the fingers of the hand, we find a group of small rivers falling into the Monnow, including the Dore in the Golden Valley, the Worm, and Escley. The Frome, a stream of considerable size, and the Leadon at Ledbury, are on the eastern side of the county.

Throughout the length and breadth of Herefordshire the scenery is extremely varied and beautiful. The broken and hilly character of its surface and its fertile soil afford endless change of prospects, embracing on every hand a wealth of vegetation, cornfields, orchards, and hop-grounds; amidst which are interspersed clusters of stately forest trees, the oak being especially noticeable from the great size and vigour of growth to which it attains. Beside the numerous rivers, the lush water-meadows are dotted over with white-faced 'Herefords,' knee-deep in pasture; and are lined with the gray foliage of the willow, reputed to have been imported into the county by Lord Coningsby, in order to furnish the necessary supply of hop-poles.

During autumn the country-side is enlivened by parties of hop-pickers, who arrive from far and near to gather in 'that most pernicious and wicked weed,' when picturesque groups of workers may be noticed around the 'cribs' and along the narrow vistas of the hop-bines. About the time of Charles I. this county became noted for fruit-growing, insomuch that Evelyn speaks of it as 'in a manner one entire orchard.' Though still famous for its cider, the production is not so great as in former years, the trees in many orchards being hoary with age, overgrown with lichens, and falling into decay. Of the cider-apple Evelyn remarks, ''Tis so wicked a fruit upon the tree as needs no Priapus for protector, since (as beautiful as 'tis to the eye) it has so cursed a taste in the mouth till it be converted into cider.'

Perhaps this country is never seen to greater advantage than in autumn, whose mellow tones add a peculiar charm to the richly-wooded landscape.

> 'No spring nor summer beauty hath such grace
> As I have seen in one autumnal face.'

Followers of the "gentle craft" still find ample occupation in the salmon-fishery of the Wye, though that prince of fishes is no longer so plentiful as formerly, when it was considered necessary to insert in the indentures of a Hereford apprentice, a clause providing that he should not be compelled to live on salmon *more* than two days in the week. The graceful warps of the salmon-fishers' nets hung out to dry on the bank, give local character to many a riverside prospect; while the coracle, that time-honoured craft of Wye-side, may occasionally be seen on the river—a light wooden framework covered with tarred canvas, in proportions not unlike a half-walnut shell, and propelled by a paddle, or carried ashore on the owner's back. Most of the before-mentioned rivers afford good sport, the usual kinds of river-fish, such as trout, pike, perch and grayling, being taken in the season.

Glancing back into history, we find the present county of Hereford and adjacent regions occupied by an ancient British people, the Essylwg, or Silures, that hardy and warlike race whose valour imposed such difficulties upon the Roman legions in their conquering progress, of which a witness exists at the present time in the numerous camps to be found all over the county. Thus it was not until A.D. 73, twenty years after Eastern Britain had submitted, that this portion of Siluria was finally subjected to the Roman power by Julius Frontinus.

During their occupation of the district, which continued some two centuries and a half, the Romans, after their manner, established themselves in the towns of Magna, close to Kenchester, and Ariconium, near the ford across the Wye at Goodrich; connecting their various stations by two roads radiating from Burrium, the present town of Usk; the one passing through Abergavenny to Kenchester and Brandon, opposite Coxwall Knoll, with a branch road from

Kenchester, passing over Frome Hill, and so to Worcester; the other through Monmouth and Ariconium to Gloucester. These roads are still traceable at many points, and elsewhere their course is indicated by such names as Stretton, Stretford, Stanford, etc., which are of frequent occurrence.

Upon the decline of the Roman power, the Silures renewed their efforts to recover independence, but after many struggles were driven back upon the mountains of Wales; and their country was ultimately incorporated with the Saxon kingdom of Mercia, under the renowned Offa, who, raising his huge dyke, created a military border by establishing a settlement of Saxons between the Severn and his new boundary. How thoroughly this change was effected is recorded in the sharply-defined transition from Saxon to Welsh-derived place-names, in passing into the country beyond the Wye. At Sutton, a few miles to the north of Hereford, King Offa built himself a fortified palace, which was the traditional scene of the murder of Ethelbert, King of the East Angles, an event of such high importance in the history of the cathedral of Hereford.

During the tenth century new troubles arose through the incursions of the Danes, who, forcing a passage up the course of the Wye, were attacked and defeated by that redoubtable Amazon Ethelfleda, who would appear to have inherited no small share of the military genius of her father, the great Alfred. Traces of these conflicts are found in such names as 'Kill-Dane Field' at Woodfield Farm, and a ravine at Amberley, to this day known as 'Woeful-Dane Bottom.'

Prominent among other leading events connected with the history of the county are the remarkable escape of Prince Edward, while prisoner of Simon de Montfort at Hereford in 1265; the battle of Mortimer's Cross, which continued from sunrise till sunset of Candlemas Day, 1461; and the stirring occurrences during the Wars of the Roses, in which the city and district took so large a share; to all of which we shall have occasion to again refer, on visiting the scenes with which they are associated.

The city of Hereford is situated almost in the centre of the county, and thus forms an admirable starting-point for exploring the district in any and every direction. The numerous roads and lines of railway radiate from the city in such wise that it may not inaptly be likened to the centre of the spider's web; and, as the artful insect can from that position most effectively survey her domains, in like manner the traveller may establish his headquarters at Hereford, and thence extend his rambles, by convenient routes, to the many scenes of varied interest to be found in the nooks and corners of this beautiful county.

The most fastidious visitor to the cathedral city will have cause to congratulate himself on his surroundings. Situated upon one of those graceful bends for which the Wye is justly famous, the city is environed on every hand by gardens and corn-fields, hop-grounds and orchards; the whole encompassed at no great distance by picturesquely-wooded hills, around whose feet the silvery curves of 'devious Vaga' enfold themselves, beneath a sky innocent of factory-smoke, and unrelieved by 'sky-signs.'

These and other causes combine to render the climate of Herefordshire exceptionally healthy, so much so, indeed, that the inhabitants not infrequently exceed the allotted span by twenty or even thirty years. Thus, in 1865, one John Price of Bishopstone died at the age of 110, enjoying to the last such exceptional vigour that he was equal to taking part in a public procession through the city no great while before his death. Again, in the reign of James I., that monarch was entertained when on a visit to this neighbourhood with a Morris-dance by ten ancient worthies, whose collective ages attained the respectable total of something over 1000 years; and, lastly, at Abbey Dore Church, in

[HEREFORD CATHEDRAL.

the Golden Valley, is a monument to a certain Elizabeth Lewis, who is *reputed* to have attained the truly patriarchal age of 141. It may be that the next decennial census will afford other examples of longevity in the district, to sustain its reputation in that direction.

Though considerably modernized of recent years since the passing of an Improvement Act for the purpose, the city of Hereford retains, in addition to the crowning glory of its historic cathedral, many and interesting traces of the past, recorded in features of greater or lesser importance throughout its older portions ; notwithstanding that so many buildings of mediæval character have been either removed or altered past recognition. The High Town was, previous to the year 1862, occupied by a timber-framed Town Hall, supported on oak pillars, the work of the famous John Abell, that 'expert carpenter' who rendered such invaluable service at the siege of the city during the Civil Wars. The old print to be seen at the Library in Broad Street shows that this was a handsome structure in its original state; but, having been sadly defaced by alterations at a later period, we can the less deplore its ultimate demolition.

The beautiful old house now occupied by Lloyd's Bank was the erstwhile Guildhall of the Butchers, sole relic of the ancient Butcher Row, which in former times occupied the site of the pleasant open square of later days. Outside, the beams are grotesquely carved with devices of heads and foliage, and within is the room of the Butchers' Guild, lined with oak panelling, dark with age and elaborately carved.

St. Peter's Church, near at hand, though modernized is the most ancient parish church in the city, having been founded A.D. 1070 by Walter De Lacy, who was accidentally killed by a fall from the battlements. The church was given by his son to the Abbey of St. Peter at Gloucester. As a result of this, the Priory of St. Guthlac was founded on the site of the present county gaol, and is described in an old MS. as 'very pleasant and large, having much land, spacious gardens and orchards, fine walks, a rivulet called Eigne running under the walls; with stately chambers and retirements, and a large and melancholy chapel, built with many descents into it from the ground, and of a great height in the roof.'

No great distance hence, passing along Widemarsh Street towards

the northern part of the city, the visitor's attention will be attracted by a group of buildings which, by their gray and venerable aspect, form an agreeable relief amidst the ever-encroaching modern streets. Entering by a stone archway, surmounted by a shield enclosed within Ionic pillars, and exhibiting on its weather-worn surface the bearings of the founder, we find ourselves in a quaint little courtyard, around three sides of which are grouped a number of small dwellings, the other side occupied by a chapel and refectory, which, with the picturesque old stone pump and occasional red-coated figure of an inmate passing by, form a charming subject for the pencil, of which our view may convey an impression.

This little establishment, known as 'Coningsby's Red-coat Hospital,' was erected A.D. 1614 by Sir Thomas Coningsby, as a charitable institution, on the site of a still earlier building of the Knights Hospitallers of St. John of Jerusalem; the latter said to be unique as a *private* military hospital. By an indenture, which bears the date A.D. 1617, Sir Thomas entitled his foundation 'Coningsby's Company of Old Servitors in the Suburbs of the City of Hereford,' the said company comprising a chaplain, corporal, and ten servitors, all of whom must be natives of the counties of Hereford, Worcester, or Salop. In order to maintain the continuity of its history, and as a mark of respect to the former governors, the founder assumed the title of 'Commander' of the Hospital, which is used in addressing the owner for the time being; and adopted the Spanish motto, 'Soies Soldathoes —Hesiathores, ne Heblathores': 'Be soldiers —doers, not talkers.'

Upon entry, each inmate was provided with 'a fustian suit of ginger colour, of a soldier-like fashion, seemly laced; a hat with a band of white, and red slippers; a soldier-like jerkin with half sleeves and a square skirt, with a moncado or Spanish cap; a soldier-like sword with a belt, to wear as he goeth abroad; a cloak of red cloth lined with baize of red, reaching to the knee; and a seemly gown to be worn, of red cloth reaching down to the ancle, lined likewise with red baize, to be worn in walks and journeys.' Although these quaint regulations are no longer strictly observed, the servitors still appear, on special occasions, in their red coats, headed by the corporal, wearing the last remaining of the original badges given by the founder. The curious wig, which formed part of the costume, has been discarded for the more useful, if less distinctive, black 'wide-awake.'

We cannot do better than avail ourselves of the guidance of the corporal, who is in command, and is always happy to place his local knowledge at the service of the visitor. The tiny dwellings look home-like and clean, each one brightened in summer-time by its diminutive garden on the quiet courtyard; showing brilliant dashes of colour with sun-flowers, nasturtiums, and lobelia against the low stone walls; and deep roofs covered with the thick stone-tiles, which show such charming tints where the lichenous growth overspreads them.

The refectory appears curiously dark and unsuitable for its original purpose; adjoining is the quiet chapel, retaining a few touches of ancient coloured glass in the windows, one end occupied by the handsome canopied pew of the founder, above which, carved in a bold manner and brilliantly coloured, appear the arms of Coningsby, supported by heraldic lions and bearing the motto, 'VESTIGIA NULLA RETRORSUM.'

Above the refectory is the infirmary, a small chamber with a curious window, by means of which those who were incapacitated from attending the chapel were enabled to take part in the service.

Passing now through an archway at the farther end of the courtyard, we enter upon a spacious garden-ground, amidst which stand all that remain of the ruins of the once famous monastery of the Black Friars. These consist of the walls and window-openings of the refectory, a few cells, and a portion of the prior's house; and last, but by no means least interesting, the open-air pulpit or preaching-cross.

This beautiful specimen of Decorated architecture is built in the form of a hexagon, rising from a flight of steps, each of the six sides having an open cinquefoil arch, supported by buttresses at the angles. In the centre rises a pillar of clustered shafts, bearing a groined roof, above which is an embattled cornice, the whole surmounted by a cross. It is very probable that the pulpit was formerly encircled by a range of cloisters to afford shelter to the people, the preacher entering the pulpit by a doorway in one side, now built up.

The little fabric having been restored no great while since, bears few traces of the five centuries that have passed over it; although the surrounding structures have long ceased to exist, including the Church of St. John, built in the reign of Edward III., who was present at the dedication of the building, accompanied by the Black Prince and no less than three archbishops.

Returning into Widemarsh Street, that name recalls the adventure of Prince Edward, afterwards King Edward I., who, when a prisoner in Hereford Castle after the battle of Lewes, succeeded in tiring out the horses of his attendants when riding on Widemarsh Common, and thus made his escape in this direction to the stronghold of his friends the Mortimers at Wigmore.

On re-entering the city, we pass at the corner of Maylord Street the site of the Angel Inn, the birthplace of that 'prince of English actors,' David Garrick, the son of a French refugee; and shortly afterwards the lofty spire of All Saints' Church appears, a notable landmark, the more so that it stands considerablv out of perpendicular. Turning sharp round to the right, near a very pretty old half-timbered house-front, we find ourselves before a weather-beaten portal, with enriched but decaying stonework, and surmounted by an embattled parapet. Entering the church, we are impressed by the well-proportioned and dignified interior; the most interesting feature being,

perhaps, the range of handsome canopied stalls of black oak, said to have appertained in olden times to the brethren of St. Anthony's

Hospital at Vienne in France, to whom are attributed certain subterranean passages and vaulted chambers, recently brought to light during some alterations at the Greyhound Hotel close by. The register of this church records the baptism of David Garrick in the year 1716.

The stalls and their 'miserere' seats are quaintly and curiously carved, bearing above them gracefully-formed canopies of delicate pierced tracery; in the vestry is a collection of ancient chained books of various dates. We would direct the attention of the *Society for the Protection of Ancient Buildings* to the impending restoration of this fine church, which in its present state is unusually interesting; it is to be hoped that the alterations will be carried out in a 'conservative' spirit.

Going straight from the church along bright and busy Broad Street, with its handsome shops and comfortable hotels, we pass into the cathedral-close, and thence get one of the most charming peeps of the noble church, with the grand porch built by Bishop Booth, itself a feature of sufficient character to arouse interest. Above and beyond rises the north transept, with its lofty, elegantly-proportioned windows and stair-turret, o'ertopped again by the broad mass of the great tower, the beauty of which is so much enhanced by the delicate ballflower ornament, relieving the breadth of surface, and clustering round the deep-set windows; the whole, mellow with the rich and varied tints of the ancient stonework and seen amidst the over-arching boughs of the elms which adorn the close, forming a *coup d'œil* not soon to be forgotten. The most interesting parts of the interior will be found in the transepts, tower-arches, and east end, the nave having been almost rebuilt, in a manner beneath criticism, after the fall of the western tower on Easter Monday, 1786. We subjoin a view of the beautiful and interesting north transept, which is seen through a lofty tower-arch, with the old pulpit and sounding-board alongside it. This part of the cathedral was built by Bishop Acquablanca—according to tradition that bishop 'whom Robin Hood robbed in the glades of merry Barnsdale.' His monument may here be seen beneath the

CHOIR STALLS, ALL SAINTS' CHURCH.

archway; it is one of the most ancient in the building, and is surmounted by a beautiful delicately-wrought canopy, carried upon slender pillars; beyond which we get a glimpse of the Cantilupe aisle, containing the tomb of that famous bishop. The arches of the triforium, here seen, are elegant and rather uncommon, and are supposed to be due to Acquablanca's foreign influence.

Close at hand is the lovely little chantry-chapel of Bishop Stanbury, elaborately ornamented with devices in stone; having a groined stone ceiling, stained-glass windows, and a pretty traceried arch opening into the adjoining aisle.

The south transept is a fine piece of Norman work, very massive and dignified; it contains somewhat of a curiosity in an ancient fireplace, unusual in such a situation.

Some venerable relics are to be seen in the aisle close by, including a small metal shrine, adorned with figures, representing St. Ethelbert, the patron saint of this cathedral, quietly performing some pious rite, while an armed figure is engaged in cutting off his head; and a small effigy in brass of the saint, who is seated on a throne, bearing his head in his hands. There are also some ancient copies of the Gospels, and a charter of Bishop Cuthwulf more than a thousand years old.

The chancel is separated from the nave by a handsome modern metal screen. It contains a sculptured figure of St. Ethelbert, close alongside of which is the handsome canopied tomb of the famous Bishop Mayo, builder of the well-known tower of Magdalen College, Oxford; who, when archdeacon of that city, was sent to Spain in order to conduct the Infanta Katharine to England, to be wedded to Prince Arthur. Beyond the high altar we notice a remarkable double arch, with a central pillar and richly-carved tympanum over it, upon which, under certain effects of light, the form of the Cross appears in shadow.

The eastern part of the cathedral, called the 'Ladye Chapel,' a beautiful example of the Early English style, is used as a parish church by the inhabitants of the parish of St. John Baptist, which surrounds the cathedral; beneath it is the crypt.

Bishop Audley's chantry adjoins the 'Ladye Chapel,' from which it is separated by a richly-carved and painted screen, with massive carved oak door and scroll hinges.

Perhaps the most curious object to be seen in this cathedral is the ancient map constructed by Richard de Haldingham about

SHRINE OF ST. ETHELBERT.

1305, known as 'Mappa Mundi.' This quaint old relic is less valuable as a topographical record than remarkable as an example of the fantastic imagination of the mediæval geographer. The artist has, however, recorded most of the cathedrals of Great Britain, although he seems to have ignored the sister isle. A very lofty Tower of Babel may be discerned, near a very Red Sea; also Rome, the Columns of Hercules, the Pyramids of Egypt, Mount Sinai, and Noah's Ark, with many another historical scene, are grouped around Jerusalem as the centre of the world.

Let not the visitor omit to climb the central tower, from whose broad summit a goodly prospect is commanded; the view extending

NORTH TRANSEPT, HEREFORD CATHEDRAL.

away from the clustering roofs and spires of the old city, and embracing the utmost confines of the county: the whole forming a scene which will quite repay the fatigue of climbing some two hundred or more steps to attain it.

HEREFORD, FROM BROOMY HILL.

STRETCHING away from the cathedral towards the Wye are grouped a number of structures of much interest and beauty. Here is the venerable College of Vicars Choral, with hall, chapel, and library surrounding a pleasant green quad, approached from the cathedral by a beautiful corridor, having open arches and curiously-carved roof-timbers; adjoining which is the site of the chapter-house, demolished during the Civil Wars, when the leaden roof was stripped of its covering, thus causing the beautiful structure to fall into decay. Hard by stand the weather-worn arches of the Bishops' Cloisters, called in former times 'Our Ladye's Arbour,' the tracery of which is gracefully elaborated; with a pretty archway opening on to the paved court where once stood the before-mentioned chapter-house; now abloom in summer days with flowering plants, which have established themselves in the interstices of the broken flag-stones. These cloisters formed a means of access between the cathedral and the bishop's palace, an ancient building pleasantly situated on the river-bank, with grassy lawns sloping to the water.

Of the old city gates the last to be removed, about a century ago, was Byester's or Bye-Street Gate, which stood where Commercial Square now is. A house in Widemarsh Street, near the line of the city wall, is still known as the Gate House; it has a fine panelled entrance-hall and staircase, with the original open fireplace and stone mantelpiece bearing the apposite inscription:

'When you sytte by ye fyre to keepe y^r^ selves warme,
Take heede leaste y^r^ tongues doe y^r^ nayboures noe harme.'

In the 'Castle Green,' Hereford possesses an exceptionally pleasant and well-arranged promenade and pleasure-ground, occupying the site of the eastern ward of the castle. The broad expanse of green turf is bordered by shady walks beneath fine groups of elms, while the centre is occupied by a gracefully proportioned stone column, erected to commemorate the naval victories of Lord Nelson, who received the freedom of the city in 1802. The attractions of the Green are greatly enhanced by the lovely and extensive views obtained, more especially

BYESTER'S GATE, FROM AN OLD PRINT.

from the terrace overlooking the Wye, spanned by its ancient bridge, to the wooded hills of Dinedor and Aconbury with their Roman camps; and the more lofty and distant heights of Garway, the Holy Mountain, the Sugar Loaf, and many another breezy eminence: the whole forming so charming a panorama that the visitor to Hereford should on no account omit to take a stroll round the Castle Green during the course of his peregrinations.

Separated only from this favourite resort by a pool of clear water, a remnant of the castle moat, is a row of lowly dwellings, built of warm-coloured sandstone; this is St. Ethelbert's Hospital, one of those ancient institutions which were so marked a feature of mediæval times. The establishment of this hospital takes us back to the thirteenth century, when the dean and chapter obtained the requisite funds (A.D. 1230) by the easy and convenient method of granting indulgences to contributors, under the license of the Bishops of Hereford, Coventry,

Salisbury and Ely. Homes were thus provided for ten ancient and decayed gentlewomen; which, with their small gardens, are much appreciated. The exterior is decorated with several pieces of quaint carving, brought from the demolished chapter-house, the one over the entrance from the street representing the patron saint carrying a model of a church in one hand, and a sword in the other.

Repassing the cathedral, a winding lane is seen leading from the

palace grounds towards the river. Here stood the cottage where 'pretty witty' Nell Gwyn was born, adjacent to the palace occupied at a later period by her grandson, Bishop Beauclerk, to whom the city is indebted for the laying out of the Castle Green.

We now make our way to the Wye Bridge, whose venerable arches were erected previously to any other bridge in the county; pausing to dwell on the noble prospect on either hand. Towards the west, where the stream stretches away in an unbroken reach of open water to the woods and lofty church-tower of Belmont, the distance is closed in by the many-folding ranges of the Black Mountains, crowned by the central peak of Pen-cader-vawr soaring to a height of 2,630 feet; a truly grand scene at sunset, when the purple ranges stand out darkly silhouetted against the splendour of the evening sky.

Turning now to the opposite hand, we have a pleasing view of the cathedral, bishop's palace, and grounds, steeply sloping to the river brink; beyond, again, the Castle Green with its bowery trees, and a graceful bend of the Wye which, before the railway existed, was frequently enlivened by the presence of the numerous barges trading up the river to the quay below the present college garden. Close at hand is the pleasure-boat station, whence craft of any size may be hired for a pull up towards Belmont, or for a lengthened expedition through the varied scenery along the lower course of the Wye.

* * * * * * *

Availing ourselves of the courteous invitation of the hon. secretary, we join the members of the Woolhope Naturalists' Field Club, in the excursion of that famous society to its 'happy hunting-ground' amidst the pleasant scenery of the limestone hills which are so marked a feature in most Herefordshire prospects. Punctually at ten o'clock of a fresh May morning we are under way, shaping our course through the suburbs, and soon catching glimpses of the river on our right. Onwards past the village of Hampton Bishop, with pretty church-turret and picturesque thatched cottages modestly hiding away amidst the embowering fruit-trees, now abloom in pink and white with kindly

MORDIFORD.

promise for autumn, braving the driving hail-storms of a much-belated spring. Another mile brings us to Mordiford Bridge, a time-worn old structure spanning the deep water-meadows of the placid-flowing Lugg, whose tide is here increased by a rapid stream coming down from the adjacent hills. This is the Pentelow brook, which rendered itself so notorious through a great flood early in the century, as thus recorded by a tablet in the porch of the church hard by: 'On Monday, the 27th of May, 1811, between the hours of five and 9 o'clock p.m., the Village of Mordiford was visited by a tremendous storm of Thunder, Lightning, Wind, and Rain, by which the little river Pentalowe was swollen in some places to an extent of 180 feet in width, with a depth of 20 feet. In passing the village it swept away a large Barn and Cider-mill, and a cottage adjoining, when William Husbands, miller, Ann Evans, his niece, Elizabeth Greenly, Widow, and her infant child were drowned just above the said village, on the road leading to Woolhope. Many hundred tons of rock were blown up and carried through the said village, by which several of the houses of the inhabitants were much injured, and the gardens nearly destroyed. A subscription was promoted for the principal sufferers, and a sum of £80 was collected and distributed among them, in proportion to their respective losses.—CHARLES JOHN BIRD, A.M., Rector of Mordiford.'

Since this temporary ebullition the stream has returned to its former dimensions, and has shown no further signs of overpassing its present restricted course. The pretty village, nestling under the finely-timbered slopes of Backbury Hill, was, 'once upon a time,' the scene of a mighty conflict between a winged dragon, or serpent, and a condemned malefactor, who was promised a free pardon on the sole condition of compassing the death of the formidable monster, which had inflicted serious loss on the good folks of the country-side. The man caused himself to be enclosed in a barrel and placed at a spot where the dragon was in the habit of coming down to drink at the river, whereupon the prisoner shot the monster with an arrow through the bung-hole; but at the same time the poisonous breath of the dying dragon, puffed through the aperture, proved fatal to his unlucky assailant. In witness of the veracity of this surprising history a huge web-footed dragon formerly appeared upon the western gable of the church, and we are told that quite recently two old village dames, espying a couple of newts of unusual size disporting themselves upon the church font, decided that they must be the progeny of this notorious monster, and at once killed them to prevent further mischief.

Times have changed since the days when iron ore was brought in barges upon the Lugg to be smelted at Tidnor Forge, now used as a flour-mill, situated in a secluded spot some two miles above Mordiford Bridge. Traces of the industry are extant in rusty castings and pieces of slag from the furnace; while the wall abutting on the river shows traces of arches for the passage of the barges, long since disused.

We now enter upon ground classic to the geological mind, and, descanting at large upon 'faults,' 'intrusions,' 'drifts,' and 'upheavals,' climb through the woods of the Haugh, site of the most ancient rocks of the locality. Descending anon to the brook, our way lies up the slopes of Backbury Hill, passing *en route* near places bearing the enigmatical, names 'clouds' and 'catstails,' amidst deep narrow glens rough with copsewood, where the bluebells are thick as a carpet, and belated primroses take heart of grace to catch the last of spring-time. After a stiff climb we come out upon the breezy, gorse-clad shoulder of the hill above a sequestered little nook which shelters the old house of Sufton, a manor held during many centuries by the present Hereford family, by the service of presenting to the king a pair of gilt spurs each time it should please his majesty to ride over Mordiford Bridge. From our present station an extensive view lies around, past the meanderings of the Wye and the Lugg through the fat lands far below, past the prominent towers and spires of the ancient city to the dark ranges bounding the remote horizon: overhead a wind-swept sky, with sunlight and shadow chasing one another across the goodly landscape. Another short pull brings us to the wooded summit, amidst the tumbled boulders known as Atom's Rocks. Once in its history was this remote eminence the scene of regal state, when King Ethelbert of East Anglia, in his progress to visit the great Offa at Sutton Walls, pitched what was to prove his last encampment on Backbury Hill, the lines of St. Ethelbert's Camp still remaining faintly traced after the lapse of a thousand years. Turning now to the inner face of the hill, a wonderful panorama is obtained of the curious geological Valley of Woolhope, with its double rampart of encircling heights, the dome-like hill of Haugh Wood occupying the centre. A prominent member of the Woolhope Club takes this fitting occasion to read a MS. paper bearing on the origin of the geological phenomena presented to view from this spot.

After certain 'provisional' arrangements for supplying the inner man, we cast a last glance around the outstretched prospect of hill and vale, and proceed on our way, clambering down by a glen where, some forty years ago, a great landslip took place, of which striking evidences appear on every hand in the broken and honeycombed character of the ground.

Descending to the plain, we rejoin our vehicles and pass through a district which has long been famous for the fine quality of hops raised within the grounds, the bines being protected from the rough gales by lofty hawthorn hedges, twelve or fourteen feet in height, which attract attention by their unusual appearance. Now comes a bridge over the little river Frome, locally pronounced 'Frummy,' scene of a disaster to the Worcester coach about thirty years since, when, early one dark winter morning, the vehicle overturned upon the bridge and, falling into the swollen river, caused the death of one passenger and injury to several others. Once more we break our journey to listen to further 'sermons in stones' at Bartestre, and then away to Lugwardine, where the members of the club are kindly entertained at tea by their hospitable ex-president, thus happily terminating a thoroughly enjoyable excursion.

THE DRAGON OF MORDIFORD.

BOSBURY AND LEDBURY.

BY the Great Western line running towards Worcester we obtain easy access to another extremely picturesque and interesting district, of which Ledbury is the principal town—a country varied by deep pastures, broken wooded heights, and numerous hop-grounds; interspersed with prosperous-looking farm-houses, each with its cluster of peaked roofs and cowls of the hop-kilns; and affording oft-recurring glimpses of the Malvern Hills, handsomely dominating the nearer landscape. Soon after we are clear of the city the train runs across the broad water-meadows beside the river Lugg, a favourite sketching ground of David Cox, the famous landscape painter, many of whose early inspirations were drawn from scenes in this locality. Here he lived for some years in a thatched cottage upon a wooded knoll overlooking the vale; the humble tenement yet stands, bearing witness to the simple habits which were characteristic of the great artist throughout his life. Approaching Stoke Edith, we get a peep at the fine mansion of the Foley family and soaring church-spire amidst the noble deer-park, stretching away up the slopes of the wooded hills to the rear; while nearer at hand appear the towers of Tarrington and Weston-Bagard: 'Lusty Tarrington, lively Stoke, beggars at Weston, thieves at Woolhope,' as the local saying goes. Alighting at Ashperton, the next station, we may push across country, past The Trumpet, a curious old wayside inn, and through Putley, with its ancient, but happily well-preserved Calvary-cross in the churchyard. Another mile will bring us to the scene of that great landslip in the sixteenth century, of which old Camden gives the following account: 'The hill which they call Marcley Hill did, in the year 1575, rouse itself, as it were, out of sleep; and for three days together moved on its vast body, with an horrible

DAVID COX (FROM A SKETCH BY THE ARTIST).

roaring noise; and overturning everything in its way, raised itself, to the great astonishment of the beholders, to an higher place.'

This event was evidently a precursor, on a grander scale, of the slip which occurred at Dormington many years back, to which we have previously alluded. In the course of its wanderings the hill carried away an ancient chapel at Kinnaston, of which the bell alone has since been found.

Retracing our steps through deep and shady lanes, anon across meadows sweet-scented with clover, where the invisible corncrake reiterates its rasping cry, we shape our course through the little hamlet of Munsley, near to the weed-grown channel of the now disused Hereford and Gloucester canal; and diverge from our course down a rough and barely distinguishable bye-lane, which brings us to Fern Farm, a remote and picturesque old homestead lying on the road to nowhere; whose deep-browed roofs, ancient weather-stained timbers, ivy-clad gables and pigeon-cot improvised from a disused barrel, form a 'bit' to make glad the heart of the sketcher.

FERN FARM.

Approaching Bosbury, we pass at Upleadon the site of one of the four Preceptories of Knights Templars in this county, the others being at Dinmore, Harewood and Garway. The now secluded village of Bosbury is a place of great antiquity, for 'Bosbury was a town before Hereford was a city,' says the local tradition, which has probably a foundation of truth in it. We find the place mentioned in records as early as the ninth century, and it appears to have been a favourite residence of the Bishops of Hereford from the earliest times, an ancient MS. recording that they 'held their state here, and dwelt in a fayre palace in the time of King Offa.' That learned antiquary Rev. John Webb thus writes of Bosbury: 'Seated in a deep but fertile country, this manor seems, from the use that was made of it, to have had its attractions and peculiar advantages, and to have been much resorted to by the occupants of the see. Everything upon the establishment was well cared for and provided at Bosbury.'

Slight remnants of the once 'fayre palace' may be traced in two sharply-pointed stone arches and inner wooden arch of the Gate-house, and the oak roof of the refectory now in the adjoining farmhouse. Here stood till recently an ancient dovecot, probably at least as old as the thirteenth century, which was unhappily destroyed a few years ago, thus leaving another gap in the record of these curious, fast-disappearing relics of mediæval times. The fine old church has a massive detached tower, standing a considerable distance from the edifice, a large half-timbered porch having the Norman pillar inside curiously cut away to make room for the holy-water stoup; and the ancient churchyard cross, spared by the Covenanters upon the rector undertaking to place upon it the words, 'Honor not the ✠, but honor God for Christ,' which may still, though not without difficulty, be deciphered. Inside the church we are attracted by several notable features; the pretty chapel erected by Sir Rowland Moreton to the memory of his wife, with quaint rebus, M on a tun, carved on the bosses; the graceful rood-screen with fan-tracery; recumbent effigies of the Harford family in the chancel; and, lastly, a very ancient font, probably of the eighth or ninth century, which was found beneath the pavement during some alterations.

The long village street, though retaining no features suggestive of its former dignity, makes a pretty picture with the homely gables of these 'abodes of ancient peace' looking out upon the tree-begirt churchyard over the way, where the sturdy tower is reputed to have been used as a place of refuge in the troublous days of old. Quite at the far end, scarce visible in our sketch, stands the wayside inn, containing, in a fine old wainscoted hall known as the Crown Room, some traces of the ancient mansion of the Harford family, whose monuments we have already discovered in the church. This fine apartment is of considerable size, with wide stone-mullioned window. The fireplace is surrounded with old blue Dutch tiles, and over it, in handsomely-carved panels, appear the arms of the families of Wrottesley, Scrope and Fox, and the date 1571. A frieze of delicate carving runs around, and at the crossing of the massive beams in the ceiling,

CHURCHYARD CROSS, BOSBURY.

three bosses show respectively the bearings of Bishop Skipp, the arms of Scrope, and of Powlett first Marquis of Westminster, having the garter and coronet.

A southerly course adown the vale of the diminutive Leadon River takes us through a country familiar in childhood to Elizabeth Barrett Browning, that sweet singer who records her early impressions of Hope End in the lines:

BOSBURY

> 'Hills, vales, woods, netted in a silver mist;
> Farms, granges, doubled up among the hills,
> And cattle grazing in the watered vales,
> And cottage chimneys, smoking from the woods,
> And cottage gardens, smelling everywhere,
> Confused with smell of orchards.'

Ere long we see before us the spire of Ledbury's great church, soaring high above the surrounding trees that cluster in rich masses upon the steep hillside above the little town. The long vista of houses rises up the hill towards the old home of the Biddulphs, itself presenting a sociable front upon the public highway—a picturesque, many-gabled house with lattice windows in the overhanging gables. Here we pass a group of time-worn tenements, where two ancient dames are taking counsel together upon the wide, steep flight of steps outside; there, a bold gable, mainly composed of great diamond-paned windows, spreads liberally into the roadway, hanging out, banner-like, its swinging sign adorned with brisk little scrolls of twisted ironwork.

In the centre of the townlet the road widens out, and here we come suddenly upon the quaint half-timbered market-house, standing upon sixteen stalwart pillars of sweet chestnut wood, brought from the once far-famed 'chace' of Malvern; and erected, as 'tis said, by that ubiquitous Elizabethan builder, John Abell.

We now turn along a narrow lane bearing evident traces of great antiquity, which leads direct to the church; affording a pretty glimpse of the detached tower and spire seen between the overhanging gables, as shown in the sketch. Ledbury Church, dedicated to St. Michael and All Angels, is a venerable and spacious structure, so ancient that Domesday Book records a priest established here at that time; and exhibiting beautiful examples of pure Norman, Early English and Decorated styles of architecture. We plunge into the interior, and find several curious and interesting features, including a Saxon hagioscope, a parvoise or chamber for the sacristan, with fireplace and holy-water stoup; some small but curious brasses, and a peculiar sun-dial formed in the glass of one of the aisle-windows.

In the great north porch we are shown the 'consecration-cross' carved in olden times upon its ancient stonework, which is pitted in numerous places with the marks where bullets have struck the wall—a reminiscence of the battle of Ledbury during the Civil Wars. In

MARKET-PLACE, LEDBURY.

April, 1645, Prince Rupert, by a forced march from Hereford, encountered the troops under Colonel Massie coming from Gloucester; when a fierce encounter took place in the streets and churchyard at Ledbury, attested by the bullet-marks still visible, and the presence of slugs and bullets lately extracted from the porch-door. The impetuous Rupert, after a hard fight, drove his adversary in retreat towards

CHURCH LANE, LEDBURY.

Gloucester; when, after resting his men for a night at Ledbury, he resumed his march in the direction of Ludlow.

But *revenons à nos moutons*. The handsomely-carved oak pulpit and reading-desk, which are the work of the late rector, the Rev. John

Jackson, were placed here in memory of his only son, who died in the year 1873. Over the altar is a painting by the late Thomas Ballard, of Ledbury, after Leonardo da Vinci's 'Last Supper.' St. Catherine's Chapel with its splendid traceried windows, was erected in honour of a certain pious lady named Catherine Audley, who lived in the reign of Edward II. Tradition records that, in consequence of a revelation that she should not abide in any place till she came to a town where the church-bells should ring of their own accord, she was satisfied that this occurred at Ledbury, where a merry peal saluted her ears while the doors were shut and no ringers were present. Here she accordingly stayed, building herself a hermitage, where she dwelt with Mabel her serving-maid, living on herbs and milk brought from a farm called The Hazel, half a mile away; the king, out of respect for her piety, granting her an annuity of £30 per annum. To this day there is a piece of land near the town called 'Catherine's Acre,' and hard by it another plot, which goes by the name of 'Mabel's Furlong.' In High Street is the hospital dedicated to St. Catherine, with an old chapel attached; and a Grammar School in the town dates from the time of Edward VI.

A curious dole, the origin of which is quite unknown, is the yearly contribution from Orlam farm of nine bushels of wheat for the benefit of the poor.

Ledbury figures in Domesday Book as 'Leide-berge,' a curiously German rendering of the name. The town belonged to the See of Hereford prior to the Norman Conquest, when the bishops had a palace here on the site of the present St. Catherine's Hospital, slight fragments of which may be traced in the wall of a cottage in Bye or Bishops' Street. A portion of the manor called 'The Hazel' having been stolen in the time of Harold, Earl of Herefordshire, was restored to the church by William I. A Saturday market was granted to the town by Stephen, on the petition of Bishop Bohun; which, falling into desuetude, was renewed by 'good Queen Bess' A.D. 1584, who granted new charters for a market to be held on Tuesdays, besides two annual fairs, the profits from which were, as is recorded in the parish register, to be given to the poor for ever.

The town of Ledbury returned two burgesses to the Parliament of 1265, but already in 1305 this ephemeral borough surrendered this privilege, the thrifty inhabitants pleading their inability to support the expense of representation.

Eastnor Castle, the princely seat of Lady Henry Somerset, lies in a hollow of the hills to the east. The 'hard highroad' would lead us around beneath Rilbury Camp, but in preference we follow an ancient pathway called 'Cabbage'—that is, Capuchin—Lane leading from Ledbury Church by a shorter but steeper route over Eastnor Hill, descending near the tiny village. The castle, though standing in a low situation, has a fine appearance, the massive walls and towers mirrored in the waters of a broad lake surrounded by trees. We turn through a gate into the wide-spreading park, and recall to memory a certain moonlight stroll in late autumn, when the hollows lay wreathed in mist, and the barking of the deer sounded weirdly through the dusk. A beautiful walk may be obtained by following the Ridgeway, that ancient British road leading to the great camp on the Herefordshire Beacon, whence on a clear day the eye ranges over many a fair county.

From this point the traveller may strike across the main road, past the pretty modern villa formerly the home of Jenny Lind, and along the breezy summit of the range, which is grooved by the dyke forming the county boundary, cut centuries ago to define certain disputed limits.

On either hand the landscape spreads afar, the level stretch of the Severn valley contrasting with the more rugged character of the Herefordshire side, where the tumbled hills range far away to the dark line of mountains which enfold the county towards the borders of Wales.

Crossing the line of the tunnel, a descent may be made by the Wych to Colwall Station, or a stout walker may prefer to push on to the Worcestershire Beacon, returning by way of the secluded villages of Cradley and Mathon. Further away in the same direction lies Bishops Frome, with its fine church and curious Elizabethan mansion, quaintly called China Court, containing some richly-panelled chambers and old paintings. By putting one's 'best foot foremost,' the railway-line may be reached either at Colwall or Ledbury, whence half an hour in the train will suffice to carry us back to Hereford.

HOP KILN NEAR HEREFORD.

HAMPTON COURT AND LEOMINSTER.

TAKING the morning train on the line running from Hereford to the North, we traverse a district of rich flat pasture-land, through which the river Lugg takes its leisurely way; and crossing the Roman road leading to Worcester, pass near to Holmer, with its detached church tower, wherein one of the bells bears the loyal inscription, 'God bless our noball King Jamese,' and the date 1609, while another announces—

> 'My roaring sound doth warning give,
> That men cannot here always live.'

Onward, through Moreton Station, where, for some time after the opening of the line, the hollow trunk of an ancient oak did service as a waiting-room. Now we get a view on our right of the flat-topped hill known as Sutton Walls, where Offa the great King of Mercia built himself a fortified palace, after his subjugation of the neighbouring country; which the Mercian rulers continued to occupy until the Heptarchy was united into one kingdom. Leland, passing this way, observed the 'notable ruines of some auncyent and great building, such time as Kenchestre stood, or els Herford was a begynning.'

Tradition records that Ethelbert, King of East Anglia, pitching his camp on Backbury Hill near Mordiford, as we have before seen, travelled thence to Sutton Walls on a visit to the court of King Offa, where he is reputed to have been treacherously murdered at the instigation of his rapacious host. His body being first laid at Marden, in the natural order of things in those days a well of clear water sprang up there, over which a church was erected, as may be seen to this day by the banks of Lugg. Ethelbert's remains were after a time removed to Hereford, when the spring which afterwards supplied the castle is said by pious tradition to have arisen. Transferred to the then rising cathedral, his shrine became an object of such veneration and miracle-working power, that the Church adopted St. Ethelbert as her patron-saint, and continued to flourish exceedingly thereafter.

Resuming our course after this digression into somewhat hazy antiquity, we quit the train at a station located beneath the far-stretching woods of Dinmore Hill. Away in the distance we catch a glimpse of Bodenham Church and village, an appanage of the Devereux family, with the graceful outline of Malvern Hills far beyond ; in the contrary direction, where the old coach-road climbs the shoulder of the hill, nestles the lonely old farmhouse of Burghope, deep in a hollow as its name implies, (' hope ' being the local term for an ascent, or slope, between the hills).

The original house was the home of the Gooderes, of whom Edward Goodere was a baronet, and sometime member for the county. Differences arising between Edward and his younger brother Samuel, the former threatened to make the property over to his nephew, a brother of Samuel Foote the dramatist. Thereupon Captain Samuel Goodere caused Edward to be kidnapped, and brought aboard a man-o'-war under his command, then lying at Bristol, where, by his orders, the luckless owner of Burghope was put to death ; after which event the house bore the evil reputation of being haunted by the uneasy spirit of the murdered man, and was eventually pulled down. The adjoining farmhouse, with its huge projecting chimney-stack and beetling gables, bears traces of antiquity; surrounded by vast over-shadowing barns, it seems in character with the sinister traditions of the spot. A story is told how a certain truculent member of this family, hearing that Sir Thomas Coningsby of Hampton Court was coming to put in a claim to the possession of Burghope, started forth on horseback armed with a naked sword, and met Sir Thomas by the way ; whereupon that valiant gentleman turned about and rode his hardest back to Hampton, hotly pursued up to his own door by the irate master of Burghope.

Upwards lies our way along the now neglected road, 'stuggy' with ankle-deep red clay, and becoming somewhat devious and uncertain among the woods: 'Oh aye, you must keep gwine up the pitch, and hold along under the coppy,' says the taciturn yokel, who is cutting gorse in a rough meadow by the hedge-side, in answer to our questions. A very warm corner this proves, amidst the sheltering boughs of the 'coppy,' now clad in the freshest green of early summer. The oaks are late this season, the young shoots showing a brilliant orange-red in the sunlight; while the open glades are bright with orchids, bluebells, primroses and, here and there, the pale yellow-green hoods of the 'lords and ladies'—a brave sight for the village children, exploring afar in this land full of wonders. From the top of the rise the road drops steeply down, affording us glimpses of 'fresh woods and pastures new,' away towards old disfranchised Leominster, a land of fine fleeces and wholesome bread; we pass by numerous cottages with snug thatched roofs and quaintly-cut yews at the little wicket-gates, more or less dimly suggestive of peacocks and other figures; while from the blossom of the overshadowing apple-trees falls a summer snow of delicate white petals.

Turning across the meadows past the little church at Dinmore,

> 'Hope under Dinmore, and if Dinmore should fall,
> The Devil would have Hope, and Dinmore and all,'

we enter a far-stretching park, and, crossing the levei turf beneath noble groups of oaks, and chestnuts in full bloom, soon come in view of perhaps the finest mansion in the county.

Hampton Court is a truly magnificent structure, combining as it does the features both of a castellated and a monastic building; surrounding a court-yard, and having a stately entrance-tower, with gateway and portcullis in the centre of the north front, of such goodly size that we may credit Sir Rowland Lenthall, its builder, who records that he had 'a little Poole made within the Toppe of his House.' At the eastern end of the mansion stands the ancient chapel, its windows 'richly dight' with beautiful old stained-glass showing the arms of the famous Sir Rowland, and of succeeding owners of the Coningsby family, easily distinguishable by the oft-repeated 'coney,' or rabbit, borne upon their shield. Among other stately apartments is the one occupied by King William III. when visiting Baron Coningsby, in which was formerly to be seen the casket containing the handkerchief wherewith Coningsby stanched the king's wound, at the battle of the Boyne. Besides works by Holbein, Lely, Vandyke and other famous masters, the present owner, J. H. Arkwright, Esq., has an interesting and valuable collection of modern drawings by Turner, David Cox and other artists—including views of the mansion as seen from beyond the river Lugg, one of which affords so charming a prospect that we have chosen it as the subject for our illustration. Sir Rowland, who came of an ancient family in this county, was knighted for his valiant conduct at Agincourt, and becoming enriched by the ransom of his prisoners 'beganne the new buildings of Hampton Court,' Henry VI. granting him license to crenellate his mansion, and to empark an estate of a thousand acres. This 'goodly mannour place' was at a later period sold to Sir Humphrey Coningsby, whose descendant Sir Thomas of that ilk founded the before-mentioned hospital, which bears his name, at Hereford, 'in thankfulness to God for his defence and protection, as well in travels by sea and land, as also against malice and practice at home.' This worthy knight appears to have been a rather eccentric character, with a somewhat hasty temper; and is reputed to have been the original of Ben Jonson's fantastic Knight Sir Puntarvolo, who is thus portrayed in the play entitled 'Every Man out of his Humour': 'A vain-glorious knight, over-Englishing his travels and wholely consecrated to singularity: the very Jacob's staff of complement: A Sir that liv'd to see the revolution of Time on most of his apparel. Of preface, good enough, but so palpable affected to his own praise that (for want of flatterers) he commends himself to the floutage of his own family. He deals upon returns and strange performances, resolving (in despight of publick derision) to stick to his

HAMPTON COURT, LEOMINSTER.

own particular Fashion, Phrase, and Gesture.' During the course of the play, Puntarvolo appearing in a complete suit of Sir Thomas's clothing (obtained by a stratagem for this purpose from Hampton Court) caused the worthy knight, who was among the audience on the occasion, to have doubts regarding his own identity; whereupon he cried out in an excited manner, 'Am *I* Sir Thomas Coningsby, or is *that* Sir Thomas Coningsby?'

The neighbouring church contains several monuments to the Coningsbys—notably, a marble sculpture attributed to Roubillac; here is also a curious MS. account of the funeral of Lady Philippa, concluding in this naïve fashion: 'And then, the next morning, hunting, hawking and good cheer, and so to continue two or three days; and such is the end of all flesh!'

The attractions of this noble residence are much enhanced by the broad expanse of verdant lawns adorned by stately cedars, and enclosing, like a gem, a dainty little pleasure-garden of formal, old-fashioned flower-beds, radiating from a fountain, with a figure in the centre. Far beyond stretches a beautiful park, some eight miles around, containing some of the loveliest sylvan scenery in the country, remarkable for the great size to which the various trees attain; here stands the Gipsy Oak, a monarch among its fellows, beneath whose vast, wide-spreading branches the deer oft shelter from the noonday heat, rubbing away the bark from a lower branch here and there, and thus causing it to die, when its shrivelled appearance lends, perhaps, added picturesqueness to the whole.

Around the southern and western flanks of the park flows, amidst pleasant solitudes, our old acquaintance the Lugg; skirting the broad valley and passing beneath the steep and wooded slopes of Dinmore Hill. Following a shady path beside the deep and rapid stream, we cross a pretty rustic bridge, suspended from the overarching trees on either bank, catching, haply, a momentary glimpse of a startled kingfisher, flashing from sunlight into shade; or the quaint, squat figure of the water-ouzel, making for the shelter of her nest.

Turning up the steep hillside, a rough scramble through a charming tangle of luxuriant undergrowth, where the bronzed crosiers of the young fern-fronds are pushing out in every direction, brings us to the level hill-top, where we call a halt to admire the rearward view across the river winding at our feet, to the roofs and towers of the great mansion; with many an acre of wild, open park-land on the heights beyond.

Tracing our way along the grassy track, we pass noiselessly beneath groups of stately beeches, when ha! there glances the ruddy figure of a squirrel, the little fellow scaling a tree so near to us that we hear the rasping of his claws upon the rough bark: now from the safe vantage of a sheltering fork he surveys the formidable intruders with bright and watchful eyes, and, on further consideration of the case, takes refuge in flight, disappearing amidst leafy seclusion. Descending hence to the road, an *al-fresco* tea is provided by the willing hostess of the Royal Oak, now cramped in her accommodation by a recent fire at the hostelry. Next arises the serious question of how to traverse the distance to Leominster in time for the evening train; but mine hostess is equal to the occasion, and the difficulty is solved by the appearance of a pathetic little turn-out, none other than a neat donkey-cart, with springs, and cushioned seat extemporized, and a youthful son of the house as driver. Away we go along the dusty road, our steed demurely trotting along in response to persuasive thwacks from his master, passing by pretty timbered cottages and the blacksmith's shop with parti-coloured doors, where the rustic craftsman plies his homely art. Anon we catch sight of Wharton Court, a fine old Jacobean mansion, anciently hight 'Waeg-faru-tun,'—the town by the side of the water-way: one of the few houses that retain traces of their original names, for there has never been a village or even a parish here, yet Wharton remains a town in the true sense of the word.

At length we reach our destination, with time well in hand, and proceed on a voyage of discovery round about the little town. Antiquaries are pretty generally in accord in deriving the name of Leominster from the great Earl Leofric, the husband of Lady Godiva, who, in the reign of Edward the Confessor, bore the style or title of 'Comes Herefordiensum,' earl or leader of the Herefordshire men. That it is one of the most ancient towns in the county there can be no doubt, history recording how Merewald, King of Mercia, built a monastery for religious virgins here in the year 658, endowing it with all the lands about the town; Henry I. further enriched the monastery, attaching it by charter to the establishment at Reading, and granting to the Benedictine monks 'freedom from all gelt and toll, and every other custom by land or water, in passing over bridges and seaports throughout England,' and many other privileges.

In the following century, Leominster shared the fate of so many of the Saxon settlements on the border, when the Britons, in one of their numerous forays, burned and destroyed a large part of the town. Rebuilt and fortified at a later date, Leominster took a large share in the wars which were of frequent occurrence on the Welsh border.

During the reign of King John the little town was again in trouble, for, during the temporary absence of the royal troops in 1207, William de Braose Lord of Brecon, and his Welsh followers, broke in upon the defenceless townsfolk, burning their priory and reducing their town once more to ashes. This De Braose appears to have been abetted in his rigorous treatment of the place by his formidable lady, described by Camden as 'that shrewd, proud, malapert and stomachful woman,' who died, the prisoner of King John, starved to death in Windsor Castle. Leominster again suffered much during the baronial wars; and after the defeat of Sir Edmund Mortimer by Owen Glendower, the latter despoiled the priory, appropriating its revenues to his own use. This venerable foundation, the earliest of its kind in England, was dissolved in the sixteenth century; the ill-fated John Glover, last of its priors, being hanged at his own gate.

Despite these numerous reverses, Leominster continued to make progress, returning burgesses to Parliament as early as the reign of Edward I.; and, thanks to the commercial enterprise of the monks, 'Lempster Market' became so famous during the thirteenth and following century, that other towns became jealous of her mercantile supremacy: and, on the joint remonstrance of Hereford and Worcester, Henry III. changed the market-day from the Saturday to the Friday, even as at this day.

In the fifteenth century the prosperity of town and priory reached its zenith, when Leland finds the place 'meetly large, with good buildings of timbre.'

Leominster was further endowed with charters and privileges by Queen Mary, at which time it was called 'the greatest market town within the county of Hereford': already, in the reign of James I., the town had acquired a great reputation for the quality of the wool of its Ryelands sheep, held in such high estimation as to be taken for the emblem of national dignity, in the woolsack of the Lord Chancellor.

A BIT OF OLD LEOMINSTER.

Says Camden, in his 'Britannicus': 'The greatest name and fame that it hath this day is of the wooll in the territories round about it; Lemster ore, they call it. Renowned is it also for wheat, and bread of the finest floure; that Lemster Bread and Weobley Ale are growne into a common Proverbe.' During the Civil Wars the ancient borough remained true to the royal cause, and was frequently the scene of local encounters between the rival parties. Sir William Waller, after the capture of Hereford, sent an account to the Parliament how he 'went to Leominster, a very malignant town, but a place of great consequence, and very rich; and having taken that town, and spent some time in disarming the malignants, placed a proper garrison there and departed.' A few years later, during his vacillating marches through this district, Charles I. twice visited the town, lying at the Unicorn Inn, now a shop in Broad Street. An insight into the condition of the country districts is afforded by a letter from Serjeant Hoskyns, who, travelling into this then remote county, gives directions that 'there must be a Hogshead of Sacke from Monmouth to Hereford, to walke with our coach. Also study the coach-way, where to break hedges, and how to avoid deep and dangerous ways.'

PRIORY CHURCH, LEOMINSTER.

Resuming our peregrinations, we traverse the quaint old streets, noting many a charming vista of time-worn buildings nodding their weather-stained gables across the narrow ways. Turning up by the new market-house, with its elaborate turret bearing the royal arms, brought from the old town-hall, we pass the small and ancient chapel in the Forbury dedicated to St. Thomas à Becket, but now converted into offices, and so come to the shady walks around the Priory church. This venerable and noble structure is of more than common interest, combining in itself the churches of the priory and the parish under one roof, and exhibiting the most striking contrasts of style, from the austere simplicity of Norman work, to the lovely windows adorned with the delicate ball-flower ornament, so characteristic of the Decorated period. Entering the church by the handsome Norman door under the western tower, we find ourselves in the original church of the priory—a nobly simple, plain and impressive interior, almost entirely devoid of ornament, with massive circular pillars and arches built of the warm-coloured sandstone of the country. One's attention is here drawn to the two tall, narrow arches, one on either side of the nave, which it is conjectured were used as processional passages. The steps to the long vanished rood-loft may be traced, and near at hand the window of the infirmary of olden times may be perceived, giving a view down into the chancel. Adjoining the Norman priory is the equally large and lofty nave of the parish church, on the site of the demolished aisle of the earlier building; beyond which, again, stands the beautiful portion erected by the parish in the fourteenth century, containing a pretty group of sedilia arches and Decorated porch, and lighted by a series of noble windows considered equal of their kind to any in the country, their stonework encrusted with the pretty ball-flower. Passing out again by another door, we cross the pleasant grounds now used by the adjoining infirmary, and trace the recently-discovered foundations of the monastery church of Saxon days, and the curious old stone coffins of probably equal antiquity.

Retrace we now our steps across the spacious churchyard, remarking the almost cathedral-like proportions of the great church, with its massive western tower and beautifully-proportioned windows. A wicket-gate gives entrance into the 'Grange,' a bright and pleasant recreation-ground, where a cricket-match is going forward upon the well-kept greensward, the children scrambling for a vantage-point atop of the Russian gun standing at a corner of the ground. Hard by appear the picturesque roofs and gables of the Grange House, now a private residence, reconstructed from the materials of the old market-

THE GRANGE-HOUSE, LEOMINSTER.

house or 'Butter-Crosse,' at the expense of J. H. Arkwright, Esq., of Hampton Court; to whom all artists owe a debt of gratitude for rescuing from oblivion one of the most beautiful bits of old English timber-building now remaining in this country. This market-house at Leominster is one of the finest specimens of the handiwork of that famous old seventeenth-century builder, John Abell, whose other houses of a similar kind at Hereford, Weobley, Kington and Brecon have been, alas! long since razed to the ground. The building is supported upon twelve massive oak pillars, having Ionic capitals and vigorously-carved brackets, with arches between them, where in former times, as seen in old engravings, the butter-market was carried on. Around the whole above the arches runs, in characteristic lettering, a curiously-worded inscription, partly in Latin, partly in English, to the following effect:

> 'Vive Deo gratus, toti mundo tumulatu.
> Crimini mundatus, semper transire paratus.
> Where Justice rule there vertu flow.
> Vive ut post vivas. Sat cito, si sat bene.
> Like collumnes doo upprop the Frabrik of
> a building, So noble Gentri doo support
> the honor of a kingdom.
> In memoria aeterna erit Justus. 1633.'

By the kind permission of the resident, we are enabled to give a sketch of the old house as seen from the grounds, and to examine in detail the wealth of quaint and curious carving in grotesque figures, foliage and heraldic devices, which encrust the old timbers on every side. In its original state the roof was adorned with four small narrow and picturesque dormer-windows, having gables above them; but, as at Hereford, these were removed by the over-cautious folk of a later time, under the mistaken impression that they injured the stability of the structure, and their materials were sold as fire-wood!

In the Bargate stands a group of almshouses for four widows, bearing on its front a tablet enclosing in a niche the figure of a man in a cocked hat and wearing but little besides, with a hatchet by his side and this legend inscribed beneath:

> 'He who gives away all before he's dead.'
> 'Let 'em take this Hatchet, and knock him on ye Head.'

Leominster has the distinction of possessing a pair of delicately-wrought silver maces, presented to the corporation by Sir Thomas Coningsby in 1618; they are emblazoned with the royal arms and the Coningsby shield and conies, and enriched with a running pattern of oak-leaves and acorns, the whole surmounted by a handsome crown on the top. Here may also be seen the last surviving specimen of a ducking or 'cucking' stool still in working order, which is shown in our sketch. Be it recorded to the credit of Leominster's fair daughters, that the last time the services of this ancient engine were found requisite was as long ago as the year 1809, when a certain Jenny Pipes was taken for a correctional dip in the river Kenwater, just outside the town. A quaint custom observed here in olden times was the ringing of the church-bell at noon on every Shrove Tuesday, to warn the housewives that it was time to begin frying their pancakes.

DUCKING-STOOL AT LEOMINSTER.

A RAMBLE THROUGH NORTH HEREFORDSHIRE.

STARTING away 'bright and early' by a morning train from Hereford, we find ourselves, by the time the Londoner is chipping his breakfast-egg, amidst broad pastures and ripening cornfields in the vicinity of Leominster.

A branch line, leading away towards the hilly west country, brings us to Kingsland Station, whence a field-path makes a short-cut to the village, whose dwellings are marshalled in pretty groups along the highroad; among which one homely front-garden is distinguished by an unusually tall tree, resembling the stone-pine of Italy, shooting up a smooth, slender stem, and bearing aloft a head of thick dark foliage.

The church, to which we next gravitate, is a large well-kept building with several features of interest. Our attention is arrested, on entering, by the so-called 'Volca Chamber,' a curious, unique little sepulchre chapel, approached by an arched opening from the porch, whence our sketch is taken. The ancient stone coffin seen beneath an elaborate open arch on the right, is conjectured to have been the burial-place of the founder of the church: it has a flat circular tablet at the foot, and a window above it gives a peep into the interior of the church. The pretty unglazed window on the east side has traceried openings of very graceful pattern.

An ancient tumulus lying between the church and the vicarage, of which the Ordnance Survey does not deign to take notice, is said to be the burial-place of King Merewald, founder of a nunnery at Leominster.

Taking up our sketching-traps, we again give preference to the pleasant field-paths, which conduct our steps to a bridge over the sleepy Lugg at Kingsland Mill, and thence jog along by-lanes, passing near Eyton Hall which, though possessing no special attractions to the artist, is famous as the birthplace of Richard Hakluyt, that curious sixteenth-century chronicler of the voyages of British explorers.

'VOLCA-CHAMBER,' KINGSLAND.

Through a rough country, we pass on to the tiny village of Yarpole, boasting another of those peculiar detached wooden church towers, of which we have noticed a finer specimen at Pembridge; then we climb the steep road under Bircher Knowl, and drop down upon Orleton, standing coyly aside in a dell, apart from the highway.

The name of Orleton has a touch of historical interest; for is it not chronicled how Adam de Orleton, Bishop of Hereford, intrigued with his patron Mortimer against King Edward?—anent whom he is credited with having composed this enigmatical anagram, of which the sense can be reversed *au plaisir* by merely varying the position of a comma:

'Edwardum occidere nolite timere bonum est.'

It was ingeniously pretended by the sender of this diabolical epistle that, if the person who received it should so place the comma as to cause the message to order the King's death, he should be held responsible for the deed.

This notorious Bishop Orleton was appointed ambassador to Philip of France, and was afterwards, through his influence with the Pope, translated to the See of Winchester.

To another Orleton worthy, Thomas Blount of the Court House, the county of Hereford owes a debt of gratitude, for the valuable researches which he made into the archæological history of the shire, the records of which have proved of so much value to later inquirers.

The old mansion, which still remains in the possession of the Blount family, has a very picturesque exterior, standing amidst a quaint, old-fashioned garden, with formal parterres and clipped yew hedges. A large panelled room is shown as one of King Charles's numerous resting-places after the battle of Worcester; in removing some panelling from the wall by the large old fireplace, the following inscription was found cut upon the stone mantel:

'Honner Him in Hart that Souffered on the Crosse for them as worship Him.'

A three-pound cannon-ball was also discovered, during some alterations, embedded in the wall. At the risk of a crick in the neck, we gaze up into the recesses of a vast old chimney, where a singular hiding-place is shown us; in which, if discovered, the luckless fugitive would certainly have met with a very warm reception.

Glancing at our sketch, a pretty latticed window which is seen above the porch belongs to the chamber occupied by the poet Pope, at the time he was paying his addresses to Miss Blount.

Adown the village street are several good half-timbered cottages, one farmhouse in particular showing a charming many-gabled front to the road, embowered in climbing plants; while overhead the moss-grown roofs are broken by weather-beaten stacks of mellow-toned brick and stone chimneys, whose 'counterfeit presentment' has, to our knowledge, adorned the walls of more than one picture-gallery.

Anent the early arrival of the cuckoo in these parts, the country folk have an old saw:

'The Cuckoo comes to Orleton Fair to buy a horse, and goes to Bron to sell it'

—the familiar cry of the bird being first noticed about the date of the fair, which is held on St. George's Day; and later on in the season, the hoarse notes are heard in the neighbourhood of 'Bron,' or Brampton Bryan.

The shadows of evening lengthen out as we pace along to our destination, beneath the wooded heights above Ludlow. The hospitable farmhouse which is to be our resting-place for to-night contains two

ORLETON COURT.

large old panelled rooms, the upper chamber having, let into the panelling above the fireplace, an oil-painting apparently by an artist of the Hogarth period; representing, in somewhat rude and grotesque fashion, the nine Muses clad in the costume of the eighteenth century, with various musical instruments; the background being occupied by a range of hills whence Pegasus may be discovered about to take wing, the cedars of Lebanon adorning the vale beneath.

Strolling into the garden—where the sweet scents of old-fashioned flowers suggest the housewife of a bygone generation, with her still-room and press of homespun linen sweet with sprigs of lavender—the path leads us to a fine example of those curious pigeon-houses which have ere now attracted notice during our peregrinations. That this one is of early date is proved by the great thickness of its stone walls; the circular roof is relieved by three pretty dormer-windows, with a lantern above, whereby its feathered inhabitants gain entrance; and the numerous holes inside can be easily reached by a revolving ladder constructed for the purpose.

In an adjoining meadow we observe traces of watercourses and fish-ponds, which, in connection with the above-mentioned pigeon-house, suggest that here was, at some past time, a monastic foundation; as the brethren were proverbial for their care in providing for the refectory table.

A bow-shot distant, perched high upon the hillside, stands the beautiful old church, whose time-weathered walls and massive, detached tower, form a picturesque group as we breast the steep approach. Some of the traceried windows are of very graceful proportions, the eastern one being of rather flamboyant character; they still contain a few traces of ancient stained-glass.

Standing in the churchyard, we gaze upon the widespread view, extending afar over woods, pastures and mellowing cornfields. Towards Ludlow, the broad glades of Hay Wood skirt the base of the hill, where in 1634, an adventure which befell the children of the Earl of Bridgwater, who lost their way and were benighted in the forest, suggested to Milton the *motif* for the 'Mask of Comus,' first performed at the castle of Ludlow in the same year.

Richard's Castle, whose scanty ivy-clad ruins closely adjoin the churchyard, was built by a certain Richard, rejoicing in the euphonious surname of Fitz-Scrob. A curious spring rises near at hand, known as the Bone Well, from the circumstance that small bones of frogs are occasionally washed out from the soil; which attracted the notice of Drayton the poet when he came this way, who remarked: 'That prodigious spring, that little fishes' bones continually doth cast out.'

Next morning we are up betimes, and bidding farewell to mine hostess at the farmstead, we pursue our way between the hedgerows; a brisk breeze driving the cloud-shadows helter-skelter across the meadows in the broad vale beneath.

In these secluded by-ways we occasionally meet a rustic arrayed in

ON BIRCHER COMMON.

the old-world smock, whose weather-stained tints give large room for conjecture as to the original colour of the elaborately-worked garment.

Hereabouts it is advisable to keep 'half an eye' upon the indispensable Ordnance Map, with whose unfailing aid we steer a course which leads us up over the broad reaches of Bircher Common; pushing our way through waving bracken, beneath stately oaks, passing an occasional quarry in the gray-brown limestone of which these hill-ranges are built.

Crossing the elevated slopes of the common, the eye commands a vast stretch of country ranging over the whole extent of our county, the horizon bounded by the graceful Titterstone Clee, the serrated line of the Malvern Hills, and the broad terraces of the Black Mountains; beyond which, gray-blue in the remote distance, soar the twin peaks of the Brecon Beacons, those monarchs of South Welsh hills.

A question elicits a direction to the shortest cut across the fields to

'Craaft,' as our rustic calls Croft Castle, which is approached by an avenue of magnificent chestnuts with mighty, curiously-twisted trunks.

The mansion, with the exception of one or two ivy-clad towers, bears no particular traces of antiquity; but the little church, whose quaint cupola appears in our sketch, and which has some good old monuments to the Croft family and antique tile pavement, is a comely little edifice.

That ancient and honourable Saxon family, the Crofts, was settled here from the time of Edward the Confessor down to the end of the last century. Espousing the cause of Harold at the Norman invasion, the Crofts of that time were banished, and their estates estreated; while at a later period, Sir Bernard and Sir Herbert à Croft, becoming aweary of worldly concerns, betook themselves to a Benedictine monastery at Douay, in Flanders.

During the Civil Wars, one of the Crofts distinguished himself by his valour at the battle of Edgehill, and elsewhere; another named Herbert Croft, who lived in the seventeenth century, was Bishop of Hereford, where his tombstone lies in the cathedral beside that of his intimate friend Dean Benson, connected by clasped hands carved upon the stones, and the legend:

> 'In vita conjuncti,
> In morte non divisi.'

The records of local history show many an episode during the long survival of this ancient family, but space will not admit of our completing the narration of their doughty deeds, so we pass on to further investigations elsewhere.

Proceeding onward through the extensive park, past grand old oaks, whose only rivals are the great Spanish chestnuts which line the park like giant sentinels, we plunge into a steep woodland path beneath a hill crowned by the British camp of Croft Ambrey, a stronghold of Ambrosius the father of Prince Arthur. A beacon formerly stood here ready against troublous times, to give warning afar in case of incursions from over the wild Welsh border to the westward.

A gamekeeper, who is setting running loops of wire along the hedge-side to catch unwary rabbits, points out the way to Aymestry, a rough footpath through a hanging wood, leading across the stream to a rustic bridge where we strike the highroad, and fall in with Her Majesty's mail, jogging demurely along in its donkey-cart.

A stone pillar at the cross-roads, a short distance hence, records the site of the eventful battle of Mortimer's Cross, fought near here in the year 1641, between Edward Duke of York, then but a youth of twenty, and the Lancastrians under Jasper More, Earl of Pembroke. The fight waged with great slaughter from sunrise till sundown, and resulted, as is well known, in the victory of the Yorkists and the capture of Owen Tudor, father of Jasper More, and eight other Lancastrians of high rank, who were marched off to Hereford and there beheaded. The story goes that a triple sun was beheld before the battle commenced, which was accepted as a favourable augury by Prince Edward, who thereafter adopted it as his cognizance.

Trudging along between the hills, which close round on every hand as we advance, we call to memory that this was one of the favourite hunting-grounds of that great geologist, the late Sir Roderick Murchison; the limestone rocks of this district yielding some of the most valuable results of his researches, which were recorded in his great work 'The Silurian System.'

A sudden turn of the road leads us past the pretty, old-fashioned Hall to the village of Wigmore, climbing somewhat steeply up the hill crowned by the church, and dominated on the western side by the ruins of the great castle of the Mortimers.

Here we bring our day's ramble to a close, and seek a lodging for the night beneath the roof of mine host of the Castle Inn; where, just at this time, the people 'most do congregate' for the testing of weights and measures, under the auspices of the newly-constituted County Council.

For centuries the great family of Mortimer dominated, with scarce a rival, the whole of this wild region, and on more than one occasion played a prominent part in the making of English history. Despite, however, their mighty record in past times, few traces survive of this bold race of chieftains, save that once dread name of Mortimer.

In the reign of Henry III., Ralph de Mortimer, who was a terribly turbulent fellow in his day, married the dark Gladys, daughter of Llewelyn, who about the same time took part in a conference at Wigmore. His son gave a welcome to Prince Edward, son of Henry III., at his castle, after the before-mentioned flight from Widemarsh.

This latter was the doughty knight who, with his three sons, held the famous tournament at Kenilworth; whence the great gatehouse was dubbed 'Mortimer's Tower.'

In the ensuing century, Roger Mortimer extended a magnificent welcome to the notorious Queen Isabella, 'the she-wolf of France,' and her son King Edward III. The career of this 'king of folly,' as Roger was called even by his own son, was brought to a tragic close in his capture by stratagem, when in company with Queen Isabella at Nottingham Castle. In spite of the queen's entreaties to 'spare the gentle Mortimer,' he was seized by order of the young king, whose authority Roger had usurped, condemned without the formality of a trial, by a parliament summoned for the purpose, and hanged on a gibbet at Tyburn, near London.

Amidst its many vicissitudes, a tragic episode in the history of this great family is touched upon in Shakespeare's 'Henry IV.':

> 'Yesternight: when, all athwart, there came
> A post from Wales, loaden with heavy news
> Whose worst was,—that the noble Mortimer,
> Leading the men of Herefordshire to fight
> Against the irregular and wild Glendower,
> Was by the rude hands of that Welshman taken,
> And a thousand of his people butchered.'

The main line of the Mortimers becoming extinct about the year 1425, Richard Plantagenet, Duke of York, now became Lord of Wigmore; and at a later period the castle was for a time the residence of another Duke of York, afterwards King Edward IV.

The most ancient record of a castle at Wigmore is of Edward's building of the tenth century; though there is reason to suppose that a border fortress existed here from the earliest times.

At the time of the Civil Wars, Wigmore Castle underwent a siege; and was ultimately, in the year 1643, dismantled by order of Colonel Massey.

Blount of Orleton, writing in the seventeenth century, says: 'Wigmore is held one of the ancientest Honours in England, and has twenty-one townships or manors that owe suit to the Honour-Court; and all the lands wherein these manors be is called Wigmore-land;

which has two High-Constables, and gives name to the whole Hundred. The abbey was founded by Hugh Mortimer, in the time of King Stephen; and had very great possessions granted it, from time to time, by that noble family. These Mortimers had great privileges, and even some Regalia, granted by our Kings to the Honour of Wigmore, as well as of life and death and of other immunities.'

The castle, whose ivy-mantled ruins we now examine, was built by William Fitz-Osborne, Earl of Hereford. Standing on a command-

WIGMORE CASTLE.

ing eminence, on the English side of Offa's Dyke—the grand natural position having been turned to the best account by the cunning mediæval engineers—and supported in the rear by Croft Castle and Richard's Castle, this was one of the strongest and most important of all the line of fortresses erected to control the Welsh frontier.

Passing through the great fourteenth-century gateway, which is in fair preservation and retains traces of a portcullis, the lofty fragments of the keep rise high overhead, a massive square pile of Norman date.

Near at hand, a depression in the ground has lately been found to lead to a series of dungeon-chambers, coeval with the work above ground.

Climbing the steep artificial mound on which the keep stands, a perfect *coup d'œil* of the neighbourhood is obtained; a green track, running athwart Jacob's Ladder Hill, being pointed out to us by an ancient smock-clad rustic as Dead-man's Lane—suggestive title—along which, in the 'good old days,' condemned prisoners were led to the place of execution.

To the northward rises the church-tower, now, alas! bereft of its quaint old bell-cote, with the roofs of the village clustering around; beyond stretches a fertile plain where, in some remote past, a broad lake once mirrored the encircling hills in its calm waters, of which a memory lingers in the name of 'Wigmore Lake.' This fair prospect is terminated by the heights of Croft Ambrey, Vinnall Hill and Bringwood Chase; which, with the 'Wigmore Rolls,' form a trilateral range enclosing the sheltered vale.

Between Wigmore and Lingen lies a stretch of rough and unfrequented country known as Deerfold Forest, where, in the early part of the fifteenth century, the much-persecuted Lollards found a refuge from their oppressors.

One of the earliest who lived and preached here was a certain William Swynderly; and subsequently Sir John Oldcastle, when pursued, fled to Deerfold, and dwelt at a place still bearing the name of Chapel-house Farm. At a spot near here may be seen a specimen of that botanical curiosity the mistletoe-oak, of Druidical fame.

TO BRAMPTON-BRYAN AND KINGTON.

STARTING afresh in the cheery morning sunshine, we take up once more 'the even tenour of our way,' casting a lingering glance behind at old Wigmore, with its castle ruins bulking bravely above the homely dwellings of the villagers. No sooner do we fairly settle down to the rigours of the highroad, than the trusty map suggests a *détour*, where a by-lane gives access to another relic of mediæval days.

Some highly-interesting remains still exist of the monastery of Augustinian canons established at Wigmore in the twelfth century; which, with the exception of the abbey-grange and the hospice, was demolished, probably at the time of the Reformation.

The noble gatehouse is entered by a lofty stone arch, beneath a timber-framed building supported, as our sketch shows, upon mighty oak brackets. Unhappily the great tithe-barn, one of the finest in the county, was burned down a few years ago. It is described in Mr. Oliver Baker's interesting 'Ludlow Town and Neighbourhood' as 'built of timber, with low side walls, and extremely high and steep roof; supported on seven principals starting from the ground, and constructed of timbers of the most gigantic size.'

The ancient 'guest-house,' now converted to the uses of a farm, retains the original open-timbered roof, albeit in somewhat forlorn condition; and a beautiful traceried window, with the old leaded panes; besides many fragments of beautiful carved work from the ancient monastic buildings.

Beneath the farmyard a great culvert has been discovered which, the country folk assure one, was in olden times a means of communication with the castle.

Previously established at Aymestry, the monastery was removed thence to Wigmore, owing to the oppression of Joce de Dinan, lord of Ludlow Castle, who was at feud with the Mortimers.

WIGMORE GRANGE.

Little is known of the history of Wigmore Abbey beyond what is recorded in Dugdale's 'Monasticon,' copied from a curious old thirteenth-century MS., written by one of the canons; wherein the old chronicler thus quaintly describes the choice of a site for their new habitation: 'It happened, one day in August, that one of the canons, whose name was Walter de Aygameth, sat in the field of Beodune among the reapers, and contemplated all the country about; and considered very attentively, and saw the place where the abbey is now situated, and marked the spot, and returned to his house, and told the abbot and his brethren what he had seen; who went with him and considered the place on all sides, and saw that the place was very large, good and convenient, to make their abbey there. And they were very joyful, and glad beyond measure, and went to Sir Hugh de Mortimer and told him what they had found, and that the place suited them well, to make a perpetual dwelling by his aid. And immediately he granted it them fully and with much joy ; and promised them his aid, and commanded immediately that they should remove thither the goods they had at Wigmore. And when they had orders to do thus, they made small delay in putting them in effect ; and built for themselves, for the time, little habitations of wood, by the aid and advice of Sir Hugh.'

During his lifetime Sir Hugh de Mortimer made numerous gifts and grants to the new abbey, including a fine gold chalice. When at length the worthy knight expired, 'full of years and honour,' one hundred poor people received during Lent a dole bequeathed by him, consisting of 'one Loaf, two Herrings and some Pottage.'

Our sketches completed, after a welcome interval for refreshment we resume our travels, passing near a place once known as the 'Treasure of Mortimer.' Crossing the highroad beneath Ostorius' Camp at Brandon, a by-path beguiles our footsteps, leading between rough hedgerows amidst a tangle of wild luxuriant undergrowth.

Before us spreads the placid vale of the Teme, with the tower of Leintwardine Church rising above the surrounding woods—a large and pretty village, much frequented for fishing and otter-hunting. Looming darkly beyond, the broad mass of hills known as Clun Forest stretches away, fold upon fold, till lost in the shades of the falling dusk ; while nearer at hand the level rays of the setting sun pick out, in brilliant touches, the rugged contours of Coxwall Knoll ; whose deeply-trenched lines of vallum and fosse conjure up to the imagination the heroic deeds of ill-starred Caradoc, in his strenuous efforts to overcome the Roman legions advancing across the Teme from Brandon Camp.

In a contrary direction, the eye is greeted by the distant hills of Deerfold, encompassing a goodly expanse of orchard and meadow land ; with a peep of pretty 'Bron' nestling snugly beneath the shadow of Brampton-Bryan Hill.

Here we bring our day's wanderings to a close, and take up our quarters for the night at the Oxford Arms, hard by the village-green.

Sallying forth betimes in the morning, we glance *en passant* at the much-restored church, and then devote our attention to the compact little ruins of Brampton-Bryan Castle, a fortress which in former times kept watch over the valley of the Teme; these are now included amidst the trimly-kept grounds of the modern residence of Robert W. D. Harley, Esq., lord of the manor.

Though the shell of the building is, as will be seen from our sketch, in a fair state of preservation, few traces have survived to indicate its ancient importance. The castle was granted by William the Norman

BRAMPTON-BRYAN CASTLE.

to his retainer Mortimer, who subsequently disposed of it to Bryan de Brampton. Eventually the fortress passed by marriage to the Harleys, a family of very ancient lineage, which can boast many eminent members, and which held the now extinct title of Earl of Oxford.

In an old record of the eleventh century, preserved at Pershore Abbey, we read that a Harley defeated the Danes at a place appropriately named Goodluck Hill; another is found accompanying Godfrey de Bouillon to the Holy Wars; while a third was instrumental in helping Prince Edward in his flight from Hereford after the battle of Lewes.

Sir Bryan Harley, son of Sir Robert and Margaret, daughter of Sir Bryan de Brampton, was a companion of the Black Prince at the battle of Crecy; and was one of the first to whom the new Order of the Garter was granted.

Coming down to Civil War times, we find another Sir Robert Harley espousing the Parliamentary cause. It was during his absence, that the castle was defended with such heroic courage by Lady Brilliana Harley, during a siege which continued some five weeks; the Royalists, under Sir William Vavasour and Colonel Lingen, eventually raising the siege upon hearing of the king's defeat before Gloucester. The brave-hearted lady only survived the struggle a few weeks.

The following spring the fortress was again invested by the Royalists, under the command of Sir Michael Woodhouse; when, after a prolonged defence by the retainers of Sir Robert, the place was ultimately taken and dismantled. As a result of these troublous times, a petition was presented to Parliament by the inhabitants of Brampton-Bryan, detailing their losses during the siege; in consequence of which a sequestration was laid upon the estates of Sir Henry Lingen. Upon the death of Sir Robert Harley, his son waited upon Lady Lingen with an inventory of the property marked for sequestration; and, after merely ascertaining that it was correct and signed by her husband, made over to her, as a free gift, the whole of the property.

The Harleys have in past times frequently represented in Parliament the boroughs of Hereford and Leominster, Robert Harley being Prime Minister in the reign of Queen Anne; the present occupant of the Hall is the representative of this time-honoured family.

But we must be up and away, for many a mile of rugged and unfrequented country lies upon our line of march to-day.

Crossing the village green, with its wide-spreading lime-tree and groups of tidy cottages, we turn south-westwards and enter the park, climbing steeply upwards by a tortuous path amidst gorse and bracken, beneath clumps of great Spanish chestnuts, now in full bloom; the somewhat unpleasant scent of the flowers being borne upon the moist air. Many a charming bit of landscape opens to view as we ascend, none the less attractive from the passing effects of 'shower and shine' which, drifting athwart the lofty hills, lead the eye away into their remote recesses, and tickle the imagination with their effect of mystery.

Striking across the brow of the hill, near 'Laugh-Lady' dingle with its wishing-well, where maidens are wont to drop pins into the clear waters with a wish for—who knows what? we come upon a woodland path above Heathy Park, and drop down by a rough cart-track into a secluded lane near Boarsford. By devious turns, uphill and down, our path meanders in free-and-easy fashion beneath the 'Devil's Ridges,' and around the broad flanks of Harley's Mountain.

The traveller hereabouts must find what solace he may in the 'pleasures of the quiet eye;' for we presume ours is no unexampled experience in trudging some five miles or more without encountering a solitary fellow-creature *en route*. However, 'tis a long lane that has no turning, and in due course we emerge upon the highroad, not far from the diminutive village of Lingen and the ruins of Limebrook Abbey.

Putting our best foot foremost, we round the base of a dark hill, bearing the sinister name of 'Hell Peak,' and descend towards the vale of the infant Lugg, by a road which affords noble glimpses of cloud-swept mountain illuminated by passing gleams and shafts of sunlight; the little town of Presteign forming a sort of human oasis, amidst this wilderness of Nature.

Upon reaching the foot of the hills we descry the ruins of Stapleton Castle, overlooking the valley from an abrupt knoll; of the once stately fabric, the walls and one handsome chimney-stack are all that have been spared.

Traversing the level plain, we cross Lugg Bridge and pass through Presteign, with its handsome church and black-and-white seventeenth-century inn; but, situated in an outlying corner of Radnorshire, the

THE RODD.

little town stands beyond the compass of our survey. We therefore press forwards towards Kington, by a route which leads us past a brace of ancient homesteads which, though lying but a short distance asunder, are separated by the brook which here forms the county boundary.

Wegnall, the first of these dwellings, is a timbered structure bearing traces of ancient panelling, which has been very badly treated by unappreciative occupants, who indeed are said to have used a large portion as firewood; the fine porch and massive entrance-door have, thus far, escaped destruction.

Just within the Herefordshire border, upon the highroad between Kington and Presteign, stands a noble specimen of a seventeenth-century manor-house; the original home of the Rodd family, whose name it bears. Built of brick and stone — with wide mullioned windows, and doorway set deep within a massive arch—the exterior of the mansion is adorned with festoons of ivy and creeping-plants; while quaint pigeon-cotes, set against the huge old chimney-stacks, add a picturesque feature.

Being courteously invited to enter by the farmer who occupies the house, we find the interior little if at all altered from its pristine state: stout oaken floors and panelled walls, wide mullioned windows, some with latticed panes; low-arched doors of black oak with curious iron latches and hinges; and, in the kitchen, a huge old open fireplace—giving an altogether old-world aspect to the interior of the mansion.

The principal rooms, which are wainscotted from floor to ceiling, contain two handsomely-carved oak mantelpieces; the lower one bearing the arms of the families of Rodd and Price. The chamber above is a truly noble apartment, with its panelled walls, deep-set mullioned window, beautifully enriched plaster ceiling and magnificent carved oak mantelpiece displaying a marvellous wealth of curious detail; of which our sketch will convey an impression, though we cannot, on so small a scale, do full justice to the intricate foliations of the carving. The figures in the panels, we need hardly say, represent Adam and Eve; while the Serpent may be discovered twining around the central pillar, amidst wreaths of fruit and foliage, with which the small triplets of pillars are also adorned.

Overhead the dragon enters largely into the design; appearing upon the oak carving, and again in the rich plaster frieze above, which leads on to the delicate enrichments of *fleurs-de-lis* and other forms, upon the beams and panels of the ceiling.

A singular feature, of which we have been unable to obtain any explanation, is the quaint pair of male figures in Jacobean costume carved in oak upon the jambs of the fireplace. Each figure is represented as bearing the left arm in a sling, while the dexter hand grasps the pointed beard; the peculiar attitude of these characteristic figures tempts us to conjecture that thereby must 'hang a tale.'

In contemplating all this luxuriant fertility of art-work, one is lost in bewilderment, marvelling how such things came to be done in this remote and comparatively inaccessible country-side, some two centuries and a half ago.

Mr. Francis R. Rodd, of Trebartha Hall, Cornwall, has courteously placed at our service some interesting facts, compiled by a relative, anent the history of this ancient family.

Originally settled at The Rodd as early, it is believed, as Saxon times, the family of Rodd, Rode, or Royd, had in after-times numerous ramifications, settled at places as wide asunder as Pembridge in this county, Rode Hall in Cheshire, Rushton and Moseley in Staffordshire, Oakhay in Devon, and Trebartha Hall in Cornwall. Camden, the sixteenth-century chronicler, mentions a Sir Hugh de Rodd as having distinguished himself at the battle of Ascalon in Palestine, during Richard I.'s crusade against Saladin. This Sir Hugh was lineally descended from Tudor Trevor, Earl of Hereford, who married a daughter of Howell Dhâ, King of South Wales. From one of the sons of Sir Hugh the lineage was transmitted—after a long interval in which the succession is uncertain—under the original territorial name to Richard Rodd of Totnes, Devonshire; who is supposed to have been the builder of the above-mentioned house, which bears the date 1629 over the entrance-door.

MANTELPIECE AT THE RODD.

The Rodds at a later period became connected through marriage with the family of Judge Pryse, or Price; whose coat-of-arms appears upon the mantelpiece, in conjunction with that of Rodd, in the sitting-room before mentioned. In 1604 William Price devised all his lands to 'Richard Rodde of Totnes, merchant; James Rodde, of the city of Hereford, mercer, and others;' to found therewith a hospital at Hereford. In pursuance of this will, James Rodde built a hospital in the year 1636, and endowed it with lands and houses; and especially with the mansion-house of the Rectory of Mansel-Lacy, Herefordshire.

The name of Rodd is now extinct in this county, the elder branch of the family being now represented by the Lanes; Juliana Rodd, grand-daughter of Judge Price and heiress of the family, having married Theophilus Lane of the Ryelands, near Leominster.

Time flying, we reluctantly bid farewell to The Rodd and its interesting associations; and pursue a narrow lane which leads along the valley, beneath the escarpments of Garraway Hill and Nash Scar. Keeping to the left, we follow a green trackway, so narrow that the luxuriant undergrowth sweeps against us as we pass; a sudden turn of the lane reveals another charming old farmstead, upon whose long, gabled front the work of successive periods may easily be traced.

The earliest portion, which is built in the favourite local manner, with timber quarterings, has a fine though mutilated timber porch, with massive, nail-studded door; and huge oak beams in the interior, where a stone stairway winds curiously around an internal chimney-flue. The farther wing was built, as an inscription records, by John Robinson, A.D. 1687, and contains a noble chamber, with lofty windows and a beautiful plaster ceiling.

Little-Brampton, as the house is called, forms part of the estate of Sir John Walsham, of Knill Court; whose duties as British minister in China necessitate his prolonged absence from this locality.

Resuming our walk, we soon reach the diminutive hamlet of Knill; perched upon a detached knoll overlooking the vale, and encompassed by the wooded hills of Burva, Herrock, and the Garraway. Crossing the stream by a footbridge, we scramble by a steep path to the top of the last-mentioned hill, and obtain from its level grassy ridge a glorious view for many miles around, which is only obstructed by some loftier heights to the westward.

Traversing the moorland runs old Offa's Dyke, which winds in a circuitous course around the side of Herrock, and passes onwards towards Titley; where it may be seen from the line, close to the station.

The path across the mountain is somewhat obscure, but a south-westerly course should be followed, which will lead past some cottages, around the shoulder of Bradnor Hill, until the town of Kington comes into sight, in the valley below. A footpath now leads steeply down, affording glimpses of the rugged scenery by which this favoured little town is surrounded.

With a glance at the well-preserved church, and interesting school-house dating from the Elizabethan period, we hasten along the busy main street, just in time to catch the evening train, which carries us swiftly back through the rich woodland scenery around Pembridge and Leominster; until the familiar landmarks of the cathedral city are discerned, silhouetted against the lemon-coloured sky of an early autumn sunset.

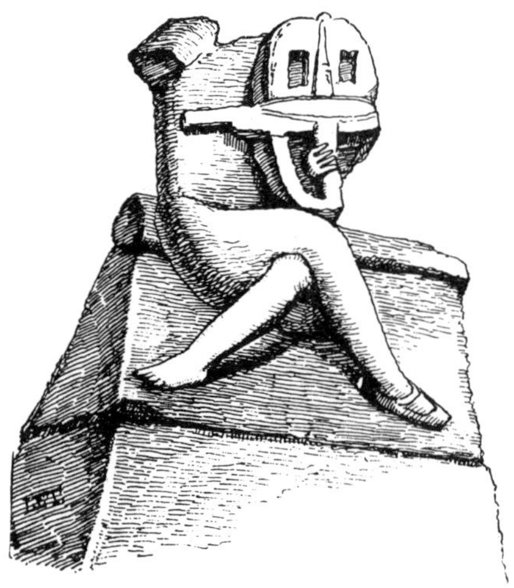

FROM A GATEWAY AT BRINSOP.

PRIOR'S MOOR, HEREFORD.

ROUND ABOUT WEOBLEY.

WESTWARD HO! A sunny June morning invites us to quit the crowded pavements and traffic-laden streets of old Hereford, for the shady hedgerows of the country lanes, now garlanded with wild-roses, and sweet with the sinuous honeysuckle; or anon to strike across the meadows, knee-deep in luxuriant growth for future harvest, and brilliant with the many-hued flowers of midsummer; scarlet poppies peeping amidst the green young wheat, whilst foxgloves and campion grace the hedge-sides. No sooner are we free of the town than we see directly before us, at the parting of the ways, the White Cross; a memorial of the time when the plague was raging in Hereford, the market then being held at this spot, instead of within the stricken city. A field-path to our right leads to the pretty group of farm-buildings and pigeon-house of Prior's Moor, the pink-washed walls of the old farmhouse making a brilliant contrast with the blue sky beyond.

Returning to the main road, we pass in another mile the King's Elm, a noble tree one hundred feet in height; and soon after come upon the flourishing and widely-known fruit and rose-growing establishment of Messrs. Cranston, at King's Acre.

Hence the coach-roads diverge, the one going through a hilly and well-timbered country to Kington, the other following the fertile valley of the Wye towards Hay—the 'Welsh Hay' as it is called in these parts.

Keeping to the former route, and passing through the pretty village with snug, well-to-do looking cottages bowery with honeysuckle and roses, and trim churchyard, a cross-road leads on the one hand to Kenchester, where the famous Roman settlement of Magna Castra once stood—coins, rings and other small articles, being occasionally turned up by the ploughshare—and thence to the site of the Roman bridge at Old Weir; the other being the road to Burghill, where the rustic porch of the little church is approached beneath the shadow of a complete avenue of dark old yews. The interior is enriched by a remarkably handsome and perfect rood-screen; and contains a curious ancient lead font, a handsome monument with alabaster figures in the chancel, and a quaint little brass let into the wall, showing the form of a globe on a pedestal, bearing the date 1619, and recording that 'Here lyeth the bodye of Robert Masters, Gent: late Lord of this Mannour, who travelled wth Thomas Candish Esqr to Virginia, and afterwards about the Globe of y^{e} whole Worlde.'

BURGHILL.

The steep wooded hill rising above the village of Credenhill is crowned with an ancient camp, probably at least as early as the remains of Roman occupation in the neighbourhood. Close at hand in the vale beneath nestles the modest church of Brinsop, with an ancient tympanum carved in stone, representing St. George and the Dragon; and a stained-glass window in the chancel in memory of the poet Wordsworth, who was a frequent visitor at Brinsop Court. This interesting mediæval manor-house was the ancestral home of the Dansey family, to whom the estate belonged for many generations, passing at a later date to the Ricardos. Of the original moated mansion the wings alone remain, showing well-proportioned pointed arches to windows and doorways; the refectory, with its massive, open-timbered roof, solid oak doors and outside stone stairway, must have once been a stately hall, though now used as a granary. During his numerous visits to Brinsop, Wordsworth wrote various sonnets

A COTTAGE HOME IN HEREFORDSHIRE.

descriptive of local scenes and events; and upon one occasion planted a cedar-tree, which has now grown to a great size, and much enhances the beauty of the garden. An interesting portrait of the poet, after Pickersgill, R.A., is preserved in the dining-room, having been presented in perpetuity to Brinsop Court by Lord Saye and Sele, as a memorial of Wordsworth's visits to the house. Of this picture we are, by the courtesy of the present occupant, enabled to give an outline sketch.

It is related that when Wordsworth's sister Dorothy was visiting here, a favourite spaniel named Prince became strongly attached to her; following her about and lying at night at the door of her chamber. Becoming by some means aware of her approaching departure, he

hid in the cart which conveyed her luggage, and met her at the coach at Hereford, when he was with difficulty persuaded to return home. Prince, growing old and infirm, became at length a burden to his friends; whereupon suggestions were made for the extinction of the poor animal. His young master, George Hutchinson, begged hard that Prince's life might be spared. These entreaties were, however, disregarded; and the dog was hanged, unknown to George,

BRINSOP COURT
HEREFORD.

by an old servant named Jerry Preece. Seeing the lad beside himself with grief when he discovered his loss, Quillinan the poet, who was at the Court at this time, wrote the following impromptu lines, which he threw out of his window to the boy in the garden beneath, calling out 'Look, George, here's an epitaph':

WORDSWORTH.

'Stop, passenger, and drop a tear,
A most ill-fated Prince lies here;
His reign, in youth, was wild and pleasant,
He hunted rabbit, hare and pheasant;
Grown old, he bid adieu to sport,
And mildly ruled at Brinsop Court;
But shame on these reforming times
Of revolutionary crimes!
This harmless, old, and good Prince royal,
Was vilely used by hands disloyal;
His noble neck was hempen-collared,
And stretched upon a willow-pollard:
O wicked traitor, Jerry Preece!
Repent, if you would die in peace.'

Resuming our travels, we have a choice of two roads by which to approach the old-world town of Weobley; one passing through the hamlets of Mansel Lacy and Yazor, beneath Ladylift, a pretty tree-clad eminence, commanding fine views of the surrounding scenery; the other and shorter route taking us by a five-mile stretch of hilly road through Wormesley, the site of a former priory of Augustine canons, founded here by Gilbert Talbot in the time of King John.

We find our road a steep one this hot summer day, but the stiff pull is rewarded by a varied prospect; ranging from the towers of distant Hereford, overtopped by the blue line of the Malvern Hills, to the picturesque heights about Ludlow, and the more remote mountains of Wales. Descending the hill, our footsteps are guided by Weobley's tall steeple, whose crumbling lines stand out clearly

WEOBLEY AND THE CLEE HILLS.

against the golden west; when a short half-hour finds us ensconced in our modest inn, a welcome haven after the day's long ramble.

From a borough town returning two burgesses to Parliament, Weobley is now sunk to the level of a village of veritable 'Sleepy Hollow' character:

> 'Poor Weobley,
> Proud people;
> Low church,
> High steeple,'

Weobley

—as the local saying has it. Happily there are still many interesting and picturesque nooks in and about the little town and its large church, bearing witness to more prosperous days in bygone times.

The manor of Wibelai was granted by William the Conqueror to that Walter de Lacy who built St. Peter's Church at Hereford; his influence must have been considerable, for we learn that he held sixty-five lordships and eighteen manors in the county of Hereford alone.

Leland, visiting Weobley about the year 1540, found here 'a market-town where is a goodly castle, but somewhat in decay;' and he also states that 'there is a fair castle of my Lord Ferrers.' The site is now only traceable by steep tree-covered mounds, and encircling moat, near which is an upright stone bearing the pathetic inscription, 'The end of the Borough, 1766.'

As early as the reign of Edward I., Weobley sent burgesses to Parliament, but this was discontinued until restored by order of the House of Commons in Charles I.'s time; after which Weobley was again represented by two members, until the year of the Reform Act, which proved the 'end of the borough'—in quite another sense—to this, as to many another 'pocket' constituency.

The erstwhile Bear Hotel, from the balcony of which the worthy candidates were wont to address the electors, now shows a forlorn and sadly degenerate front to the street; its many chambers silent and deserted, and the great doors ever closed.

It is much to be regretted that the fine market-house, built by that local celebrity, John Abell, has shared the fate of so many of these ancient structures, having been pulled down some five-and-forty years ago; the large and handsomely-proportioned building adjoining has, however, fortunately been spared; a structure whose interest is, perhaps, enhanced from the fact that it was formerly the abode of one Tomkins, of whom it is recorded in a sonnet written in his honour that he was 'the father of thirty-two children born in one chamber at Weobley'—we need, therefore, scarcely offer an apology for giving a view of this famous dwelling.

In September, 1645, Weobley received a hasty visit from King Charles I., during a march continued from early morning till midnight. During his halt at the Crown Inn, he might perchance be reminded of

WEOBLEY.

old Camden's saying, 'Lemster bread and Weobley ale are grown into a common proverbe.' The house, though no longer an inn, is called in commemoration of this visit the Throne Farm, where the room occupied by the royal guest is still pointed out. Across the road, the visitor's attention will be drawn to the charming little half-timbered front of the old school-house, with projecting porch and carved spandrels; now uninhabited, and the doorway hedged across by trailing sprays of neglected rosebushes, recalling in its humble way the palace of the Sleeping Beauty. It is devoutly to be hoped that this characteristic remnant of old Weobley may be preserved from untimely destruction.

OLD STREET AT WEOBLEY.

A few steps away, near Jack-leg Lane, a heap of stones marks the dwelling-place of an ancient inhabitant, whose house had grown so dilapidated that it was found necessary to pull it down, only a small part being left; yet, so strong was the old man's affection for his 'ain fireside,' that he was wont to sit by the ruinous hearth under the shelter of a capacious umbrella!

At the lower end of the town stands the large and interesting church of SS. Peter and Paul, the fine tower and spire being a conspicuous feature in the landscape, from whichever direction the town is approached. The earliest portions are probably the porch, and a piscina of the eleventh century; there are examples of thirteenth-century work in the nave and chancel, but the greater part is of a century later.

Bishop Orleton, in 1325, dedicated the church of Webbelye and three altars therein; one of them was doubtless in the chapel of St. Nicholas, which belonged to the family of Bridges of 'the Ley.' All lovers of old work will regret that the handsome screen, which once enclosed this and the adjoining 'Monnington' chapel, was removed during the 'restoration' which befell the church in 1868, one post alone remaining to recall the loss sustained in this entirely senseless alteration. In the chancel stands a fine full-length marble statue of Colonel Birch, sometime member for Weobley, beneath a handsome Corinthian canopy, with inscription setting forth the virtues and achievements of that redoubtable Parliamentary soldier who, after capturing Hereford by a successful ruse, was made governor of the city by Cromwell.

This remarkable man began life as a packhorse driver, thus acquiring the intimate knowledge of the country which proved of the utmost service to him during his military career. It is related that, while plying his trade, he fell in with a band of Roundhead soldiers, who attempted to rob him of his goods; when he defended himself so valiantly that, upon hearing of the affair, Cromwell offered him a commission in his troop, and subsequently promoted him to a high command. Becoming enriched by his astute management of his own affairs, and more peaceful times ensuing, Colonel Birch lived for many years at 'the Homme,' near Weobley; and in the year 1661 purchased the fine estate of Garnstone from a member of the Tomkins family, and, after representing the borough of Weobley in Parliament, died here in 1691.

Near to the statue of this famous soldier are two fine table monuments of good design, the one being that of Sir Walter Devereux, who

OLD SCHOOL HOUSE AT WEOBLEY.

died in 1402; the other probably representing Sir John Marbury and his wife Agnes, who died in 1437 and 1433 respectively; and it is conjectured that the latter monument conceals the tombstone of Sir Hugh de Lacy, founder of Llanthony Priory in Monmouthshire, and in all probability the original builder of Weobley Church.

The climb up the lofty tower is rewarded by a wide-stretching view over broken and fertile landscapes, with here and there a peep of the hop-yards and pointed roofs of the kilns; in autumn enlivened by the presence of numerous parties of hop-pickers from all the countryside. Bowery orchards surround the cottages, where the little town, with its

WEOBLEY MARSH.

timber-framed gables and venerable stone-tiled roofs, bronzed by the bright-coloured lichens, lies spread like a map at our feet.

The pleasant prospect spreads away over hill and vale, where quiet, secluded villages nestle by the wayside, to the rugged escarpments of the Black Mountains, rising cliff-like above the fertile Valley of the Wye; the distant Clee Hills bound the scene far to the north, while towards the east the eye ranges over the wooded and picturesque country lying about Garnstone Park, terminated by the graceful outline of Ladylift.

A short half-mile across the upland meadows, where the hedgerows are now in all their summer glory of honeysuckle and wild-rose, will bring us out upon the 'plock'—as such a piece of rough ground is here called—over against that fine old timbered mansion called 'the Ley,' which is, perhaps, responsible for the latter half of the name of Weobley. According to Blount, 'this is a gentil habitation in the parish of Weobley, and was anciently a village, where a family that bore name from the place had an interest. In the beginning of Henry VI.'s time Richard de Ley, for want of issue male, left the estate to his daughters Margaret and Mariot, of whom Simon de Brugge, in Bridge Solers, purchased it.'

This family were benefactors of the neighbouring monastery of Wormesley. The estate remained in the hands of the De Brugges until granted to Roger, Lord Clifford, owing to the adherence of Simon de Brugge to Simon de Montfort and the rebel barons; but, by the 'Dictum de Kenilworth,' these lands were restored to their former owners. Sir John de Brugge was present at the battle of Agincourt; Sheriff of Herefordshire in 1417; and subsequently one of the members for the county.

The present mansion occupies the site of an older house, and is a beautiful example of the timber dwelling of the English yeoman of the sixteenth century; with its finely carved beams, ornamental plaster work, and diamond-paned windows. A charming feature is the boldly projecting entrance-porch, which has a massive nail-studded door, and over it the quaint device and motto of the founder, bearing the date 1589. The interior has been modernized to such an extent as to have lost any character which it may once have possessed. The Ley now forms part of the Garnstone estate, and is used as a farmhouse.

An interesting story is told of the great Lord Eldon's connection with Weobley. In 1783, when, as plain Mr. John Scott, he first became candidate for this borough, he was received at the house of Mr. Bridge, the clergyman; who, having a daughter then a young child, extracted a jocular promise from him that, if ever he should become Chancellor, and the little girl's husband should happen to

WEOBLEY
HEREFORDSH

be a parson, the Chancellor would give that parson a living. The sequel, partly related by Lord Eldon himself to his niece, Mrs. Forster, was as follows: after referring to his original promise, he proceeds:—'Years rolled on, I came into office, when one morning I was told that a young lady wished to speak to me, and I replied that young ladies must be attended to, so they must show her up; when up came a very pretty young lady, who curtsied and said she thought I did not recollect her. I answered I certainly did not, but perhaps she could recall herself to my memory. So she asked if I remembered the clergyman at Weobley, and his little girl, to whom I made a promise. "Oh yes," I said, "I do; and I suppose you are the little girl?" She curtsied and said, "Yes." "And I suppose you are married to a clergyman?" "No," she said, blushing, "but I am *going* to be married to one, if you, my lord, will give him a living." Well, I told her to come back in a few days, when I made inquiries to ascertain from the bishop of the diocese that the gentleman she was going to marry was a respectable clergyman of the Church of

England; and then I looked at my list, and found I actually had a living vacant which I could give him. So when the young lady came back, I told her she might return home and get married as fast as she liked, for her intended husband should be presented to a living, and I would send the papers as soon as they could be made out. "Oh no!" she exclaimed, and again blushed and curtsied; "pray, my lord, let me take them back myself." I was a good deal amused; so I had the papers made out, and signed them, and she took

GARNSTONE CASTLE.

them back the next day. Is it not remarkable that I should have given that promise in early life, and that it should actually have been fulfilled?'

Weobley's lordly neighbour, the stately castellated mansion of Garnstone, may be approached by a field-path direct from the village, passing beside the grass-grown mounds of the castle, and through open meadows extending to the verge of the park, where noble groups of oak, elm and Scotch fir, are relieved by the level spreading boughs of an occasional cedar.

The present mansion, built by Nash, occupies the site of an earlier house, in which Colonel Birch resided until his death; to whose descendants the estate belonged until, in 1752, the property passed

I·B
1589
IN DEI NOMINE
"THE LEY" HEREFORDSHIRE

to Dr. Samuel Peploe, Archdeacon of Richmond and Warden of Manchester, from whom it has descended to its present owner.

Our ramble may very well be extended to the summit of Ladylift for a charming peep of the towers and spires of Hereford; or we may pass through Wormesley, the site of a priory of Augustinian canons, and examine the curious and picturesque pigeon-house at the Buttas.

This quaint little building, the handsomest of its kind in the county, is richly carved with a running pattern, in which figures alternate with foliage; it stands near a large old farmhouse, in a curiously out-of-the-way situation, upon an eminence whence, on a clear day, a fine prospect is obtained, embracing a rich country bounded by the Malvern Hills. This pigeon-house was erected by George and Elizabeth Karver, whose initials appear in raised panels on the front, with the date 1632, and is locally reputed to have also been used as a falconry. It is said that the wooded hill close by, called 'Robin Hood's Butts,' was frequented by that famous archer to shoot his arrows across to Canon Pyon Hill; but, as the latter is a full mile away, the story must assuredly be accepted *cum grano salis.*

The return to Weobley may be varied by taking the pretty village of King's Pyon *en route*, where the church is said to be roofed with Irish timber, and contains a fine monument bearing the arms of the Mortimers, the former lords of this manor.

Another delightful stroll of about two miles across open meadows, where the cattle are grazing half hidden in the deep pasture, leads us by pleasant paths to the village of Dilwyn; prettily situated in a hollow, near the ancient Watling Street. The massive tower and wooden spire of the venerable church rise gracefully above the village, standing amidst the well-tended churchyard where, surely, 'the rude forefathers of the hamlet' must rest in peaceful seclusion. By a large stone porch we enter an interior which, in our estimation, is extremely interesting, bearing traces of numerous alterations in past times.

Curious it is to note in what a daring way the great tower arch has been built against, in widening the church, and the ancient windows of the clerestory blocked up and replaced by others of a later style.

PIGEON-HOUSE AT THE BUTTAS.

The Luntley Chapel is separated from the nave by a massive but roughly executed screen, probably the handiwork of some local village carpenter. In the chancel we are attracted by the recumbent figure of a Crusader, whose attitude implies that he had paid as many as three visits to the Holy Land during his career.

Beyond the hills to the westward, lies the picturesque timber-framed manor-house of Luntley, with spacious open porch, supported on an arcade of oaken pillars, and showing many pretty bits of carved work here and there: the four-gabled pigeon-house standing in an adjoining meadow bears the date 1673. There is little doubt that this house, to

LUNTLEY MANOR-HOUSE.

which the before-mentioned chapel was attached, was in former times a place of some importance, though now used merely as a farmhouse.

Rambling through bye-lanes towards Pembridge, a pleasant little interlude occurs, when we call at a wayside farm, where our ancient, but hospitable hostess conducts us to her spacious 'house-place;' where, ensconced in a roomy settle, she regales us with wholesome home-made wine, and a chat about old customs of the country-side, now all too rapidly falling into disuse. Anent a certain mysterious bunch of hawthorn twigs depending from a beam of the ceiling 'hangs a tale.' Early on New Year's morning, the men and boys employed at neighbouring farms meet in a field, where they tie bundles of straw together on a long pole; then, after setting the straw alight, a man runs off with it over twelve fields sown with wheat, while the bystanders shout aloud, 'Old Cider! old Cider! old Cider! Brave old Cider! Three times three, hurrah!' When the man has run his course, the straw is overhauled, and should it have ceased to burn, this is considered to augur ill-luck for the crop. The same morning the mistletoe and hawthorn- or blackthorn-bush, which have hung in each house during the past year, are taken down, and fresh branches put up for the coming twelvemonth. In order to make it supple, the blackthorn branch is burnt over the fire and then twisted into a wreath; and, finally, men and boys are feasted, and the day is kept as a holiday.

In olden times the custom of 'wassailing' was observed in these parts, when a cake was made and placed on a bullock's horn whilst standing in the stall; the animal was then pricked with a prong, which caused him to toss his head; whereupon, should the cake be thrown into the trough, or 'boosey,' in front of him, it went to the bailiff; but if it fell behind the bullock, then it was claimed by the farm lads. Wassail was then held, a bucket of cider being passed round, and the master's health drunk to the following verse:

> 'Here's to the champion of the white horn;
> Here's God send the master a good crop of corn,
> Of wheat, rye and barley, and all sorts of grain:
> If we live to this time twelvemonth, we'll drink his health again.'

Bidding farewell to our communicative hostess, we trudge merrily on and, turning a sharp corner, come suddenly upon the little town of Pembridge; sedately ensconced in a quiet nook near a pretty stream called Arrow. Right before us stands an ancient hostelry, with overhanging gables, whose equally venerable *vis-à-vis* is the timber-built market-place where, at hiring fairs, the lads and lassies are wont to take their stand. Espying an angle of the church hard by, we climb a flight of stone steps leading to the churchyard, and visit the curious and almost unique detached belfry.

This quaint and interesting old structure was built in the fourteenth century; the lower part of stone, of an octagonal form, the upper

PEMBRIDGE.

portion of wood, supported on four huge massive timber posts, each consisting of a single tree-trunk, giving to the inside of the tower all the appearanceof a barn; it contains a peal of bells and a clock.

We notice many of the familiar black-and-white house-fronts, and remark the number of old tenements, both in the villages and by the lane-sides, which are, unhappily, void; affording striking proof of the gradual decrease of the rural population, a fact so forcibly illustrated by the recent census returns.

At the town end we pause to glance at the group of modest almshouses erected by the Rev. Thomas Trafford, D.D., for six aged women and endowed by his widow, as recorded on the first cottage; the one at the opposite end bearing a board announcing that 'This Hospitoll was bielded by me, Thomas Powle, carpenter, according to the donor's will, in 1686.'

BELFRY AT PEMBRIDGE.

Free of the houses, we take to the field-paths, and so 'go merrily hent the stile-a,' passing through broad meadows, where the haymakers are working full-tides this hot July day; and ere long come to Eardisland, a bright, pleasant village, through which the river Arrow meanders in a clear stream, running here over rippling shallows, anon into shady pools,

> 'With here and there a lusty trout,
> And here and there a grayling.'

The bridge and neighbouring pigeon-house, with a metal fish as weather-vane, group in a very charming manner, with a replica in the placid waters of the stream.

Away in the west the gathering clouds look ominous, and at length the threatened storm breaks across the country, driving us to the shelter of a hospitable roof, when, ensconced in a cosy oak settle, we watch the tumult of the elements with what patience we may; noting the wild gesticulations of the wind-lashed branches, and how the torrents of heavy rain fleck the surface of the stream with a myriad dancing motes. Anon the crackling thunder breaks overhead, reverberating around the sky in majestic tones that might shame the grandest organ-peal. More wild gusts ensue, and at length the storm sweeps away in a watery veil, through which the rainbow gleams.

The weather improving towards sundown, we start afresh, walking delicately after the manner of Agag, and picking our steps along the drenched roadway, as the west becomes golden beyond the cumulus clouds low upon the horizon, and the retreating storm-wrack is suffused with a rosy glow. The lane becomes a veritable avenue beneath the broad-limbed oaks, as we approach Burton Court, with its quaint little pigeon-house of timber and stonework. As we enter the main road a group of trees attracts us by its curious appearance, a pair of ancient yews growing beside three great Spanish chestnut-trees which spring from one parent stem—a very uncommon sight.

Pushing onward in the gloaming, the *clack-clack* of a belated grass-mower comes faintly across the meadows, and now we catch a distant glimpse of Weobley's tall steeple, beyond the nearer spire of Dilwyn; a sharp turn down hill takes us through the village, and so by more field-paths we enter Weobley, as the labourer is plodding homeward, pipe in mouth, from his day's work upon the plough lands, or amidst the far-stretching avenues of the hop-yards.

FROM WEOBLEY TO HAY.

ONCE more turning our faces towards the setting sun, we make our way, zigzag fashion, up the broad Valley of the Wye to the confines of the county; noting many characteristic features amidst the rural district through which our journey lies.

Upon quitting the grass-grown streets of Weobley, we soon strike a field-path through meadows which, in early autumn, are empurpled with the delicate flowers of the leafless crocus. This path brings us out into a lane near the eighteenth-century brick mansion of Sarnesfield, close to the point where two old coachroads into Wales cross one another. The tiny plot of land here 'islanded' between the roadways, is held under the curious condition that the proprietor must drive round the ground once a year—easy terms indeed to the local owner.

Beside the diminutive church of Sarnesfield, which lies hidden away amidst trees in a dingle, may be seen the weather-worn monument of John Abell, the famous Herefordshire architect; carved by his own hand when ninety years of age, with quaint figures representing himself and his two wives, bearing the emblems of his profession, and this very characteristic legend:

> 'This craggy stone a covering is for an architect's bed,
> That lofty buildings rais'd high, yet now lies low his head;
> His line and rule, so death concludes, are locked up in store:
> Build they who list or they who wist, for he can build no more.
>
> His house of clay will hold no longer,
> May heaven's joy build him a stronger.'

John Abell was the builder of the town-halls at Hereford, Kington and Brecon, and of the market-houses at Weobley and Leominster; all of which have, unfortunately, been taken down with the exception of the last, which has happily been rescued from destruction and rebuilt on another site, through the liberality of a local resident.

For his services during the siege of Hereford, Abell was honoured by Charles I. with the title of 'one of his Majesty's carpenters.' Governor Scudamore, in a despatch to Lord Digby, refers to him as 'an expert carpenter, the only man in all this country to make mills; without whom we had been much disfurnisht of our means to make powder (after our powder mill was burnt), or grind corne.' John Abell died in 1691, in the ninety-seventh year of his age.

At Kynnersley, near Sarnesfield, stands the curious castle of the Delaberes, a structure of stone and brick of the reign of James I., with crow-stepped gables. The church, which is close at hand, contains a singular reredos, with elaborate panels carved and gilt; the pulpit also has figures carved in oak of good design; indeed the whole interior will well repay investigation. At the west end is the curiously plain and simple, but well-proportioned tower.

Passing hence through the adjoining village of Eardisley, where we find some slight remains of a castle which was held for some centuries by the ancient family of Baskerville, we approach the Wye once more, near a quaint wooden bridge and disused toll-house;

and diverging for a mile or so, we settle down for a sketch of Rhydspence, an interesting, half-timbered wayside hostelry, situated on the confines of England and Wales, whence a fine view is obtained across the broad valley.

Sketches completed, we 'up sticks and away,' crossing the rapid stream below the old inn by a crazy old ferry-boat, and climbing to the bank by a path which leads across the meadows towards a wooded eminence. The landscape in this locality is charmingly diversified, lofty wooded hills rising abruptly from the riverside, the one in front crowned by the ruins of Clifford Castle, surmounting a rugged face of rock which here sweeps down to a shingly bend of the Wye.

It is recorded at the time of Domesday Book that one Drogo had a son named Richard, who married Maud de Toney, and received Clifford Castle as his wife's dowery; their son Walter thus assumed the name of De Clifford, and was the father of Joan de Clifford, the 'Fair Rosamond' whose beauty and tragic fate have been sung in many a romance, and who spent her early days in comparative seclusion within these walls.

In the stormy days of Norman and Plantagenet, the noble family of De Clifford ranked among the great barons of the realm, and held extensive possessions upon the marches of Wales :

> 'Here in the shade of age-worn Hatterel
> A Rose once bloomed, soon by the torrid blast
> Of jealous hatred withered.
>
> * * * * *
>
> The ruined arch and fall'n parapet
> With weeds o'errun, these only mark the place
> Which echoed once with princely revelry ;
> Clifford long since hath lost its ancient race.'

Of the castle, erected by William Fitz-Osborne in the eleventh century, considerable fragments still remain ; from whose ivy-mantled embrasures an extensive view is obtained of the sinuous course of the river and surrounding heights, dominated by the Hatterel Hills about Hay, and the Black Mountains in Wales.

RHYDSPENCE INN.

Ascending the hill past the scattered village, we enter the churchyard and pass on to the church, which will repay examination, having some Norman features as well as traces of later periods, and a few interesting monuments to the De Cliffords.

A pleasant field-path leads hence beneath noble groups of beeches to the priory, where an oak-tree of unusual size attracts our notice; presently we join the highroad, passing beneath a wooded hill whose summit is crowned by an early British camp known as Mouse Castle, one of the strongest though smallest of its kind in the county. Another mile and we enter the little border town of Hay, perched upon the steep bank of the Wye.

The Welsh Hay, as this town is commonly called, overlooks the vale at a point where the river enters the county of Hereford, after its tortuous course amid the wild hills of Central Wales.

Besides the so-called castle, there are not many features of sufficient interest to detain us long in the border town of Hay.

Of the mediæval castle founded by Philip Walwyn, who received the manor of Hay from Bernard de Newmarch, a tower and fine arched gateway, built by Humphrey Bohun, Earl of Hereford, alone remain; a later portion of Jacobean date having been converted to the purposes of a dwelling-house, which is now the residence of the Rector of Hay.

Many are the vicissitudes through which this old castle has passed; the original structure having been demolished in Henry II.'s time, and afterwards rebuilt by Maud de la Haie, wife of William de Breos. So rapidly was the work carried out by the enforced labour of this lady's dependents, that a story went abroad, which crystallized in course of time into the legend of Maud de la Haie carrying stones in her apron, and rebuilding the castle in a single night. Eventually the fortress was demolished by Owen Glendower, that redoubtable scourge of the march lands.

The church, having been rebuilt in the 'churchwarden' period, is, to say the least, unattractive; but possesses some ancient plate dedicated to 'Our Lady Paris of the Haie.' Closely adjoining the edifice a grass-grown tumulus may be noticed—a relic of prehistoric antiquity; and

OLD MARKET-HOUSE, HAY.

nearer the station some slight traces exist of Roman walling, built up with later work.

Hay will be found a good starting-point for several pleasant rambles: by following the course of the Dulas-brook, for instance, we may visit Cusop, with its little mountain church shaded by venerable yew-trees, whence, passing through a narrow dingle, a good walker may range across the hills and penetrate the secluded Olchon glen; or may follow the mountain road to Llanthony, where he will be glad to find homely but comfortable quarters within the precincts of the ruined priory.

At Hay, too, we are in touch with the Golden Valley district, by means of the local railway which runs hence to Pontrilas, passing through some interesting localities which are described in another chapter. For the present, however, we will rest awhile after our extended rambles, and avail ourselves of an evening train to return to Hereford.

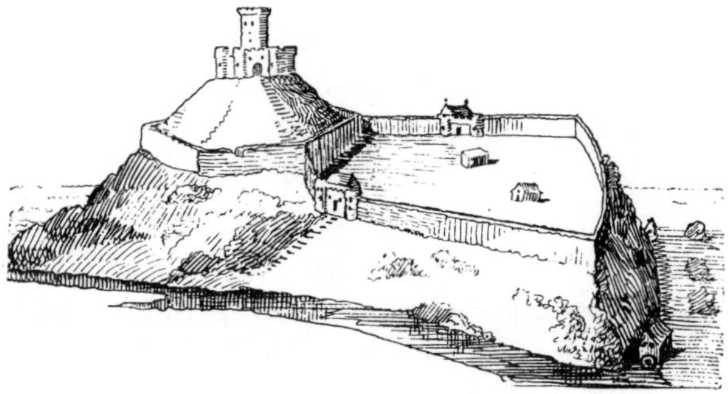

HEREFORD CASTLE, FROM AN OLD PRINT.

PONTRILAS, AND THE GOLDEN VALLEY.

'Where the broken landscape, by degrees
Ascending, roughens into rigid hills ;
O'er which the Cambrian Mountains, like fair clouds
That skirt the blue horizon, dusky rise.'

THESE lines very happily epitomize the salient features of the landscape, as we approach the south-western borders of Herefordshire ; where, amidst some of the finest scenery to be found in the county, many charming nooks may be discovered, replete with subjects to delight the artist, the antiquarian, or the traveller—like Dr. Syntax—in search of the picturesque ; who can here enjoy 'the pleasures of the quiet eye,' in undisturbed seclusion.

Once more turning our back upon the cathedral city, we cross the rapid-flowing Wye by a mediæval bridge, and, gradually ascending, obtain a pretty vista of tower and spires ; near at hand the tower of the beautiful modern Roman Catholic cathedral of Belmont is seen, placed on a fine ascent close to the river.

Away beyond lies Clehonger, where the Aubrey Chapel contains some handsome monuments to the family of that name. Erelong we come to Allensmore, situated in a district which, from being a tract of waste land on the confines of Haywood Forest, was reclaimed by Alan, Lord of Kilpeck ; who appears to have been an ardent agriculturist of his time, to the benefit of Alan's-moor.

Onwards ! the scenery becoming ever of a more varied character as we advance, the heights of Aconbury, Orcop, and Saddlebow hills showing a broken outline ahead.

Rounding the skirts of the wooded 'valletts' at Thruxton, another mile takes us by St. Devereux, where we cross the railway bridge, and soon find our way by a pleasant field-path to our destination, the little village of Kilpeck. The small but exceptionally interesting church stands upon a slight eminence overlooking a rolling, broken country, watered by the rivulets from the adjacent hills. The whole neighbourhood is highly picturesque and fertile. Close to the village and church stand the ruins of the castle, from whose lofty mounds a charming view is

KILPECK.

obtained across broad, level meadows of unrivalled verdure, almost entirely unacquainted with the ploughshare, and separated by leafy hedges and deep dingles; the prospect embracing the massive steeps of Hatterel Hill, and the finely-timbered slopes of Garway.

'Chilpecte in Irchenfield' was, at the time of Domesday Book, the home of William Fitz-Norman; whose descendant, Hugh of that ilk, to whom the castle was granted at the time of the Conquest, gave the present church and the chapel of St. Mary, then standing within the castle, to the church of St. Peter at Gloucester; where we find them included in the charter granted to the corporation by King Stephen in 1138, and in other charters of a later date.

Of the Benedictine priory once existing here, but suppressed in 1422, the site only remains; its foundation is attributed to Hugh Fitz-Norman, from whom it received various endowments, and was subordinate to St. Peter's, at Gloucester.

KILPECK CHURCH.

William de Cantilupe, a great border baron of King John's time, had the honour of entertaining his sovereign on several occasions at Kilpeck Castle. This fortress came, after various vicissitudes, into the possession of Sir William Herbert, first Earl of Pembroke, in the reign of Edward IV., to whom it was presented in reward for his valuable services in upholding the fortunes of the House of York.

During a tough fight at Edgecote, near Banbury, when his Welshmen were seized with panic and routed, this valiant knight was taken

NORMAN DOORWAY, KILPECK CHURCH.

prisoner, and was ultimately beheaded at Northampton by order of Richard Neville, Earl of Warwick.

Kilpeck castle was afterwards restored by Edward IV. to John, Earl of Ormonde, who stood so high in the estimation of his king that he

INTERIOR OF KILPECK CHURCH.

spoke of the earl as 'the goodliest knight he ever beheld, and the finest gentleman in Christendom.'

After exploring the scanty remnants of the castle, and admiring the extensive view from its grassy slopes (which were in olden times protected on the Welsh side by a chain of lakelets), we descend to the church, a stone's-throw distant. The south door by which we enter is almost unrivalled in the curious and elaborate character of its sculpture; the Serpent enters largely into the design, appearing on the right-hand side in the act of climbing the Tree of Knowledge, of which, it will be observed in the sketch, Adam is partaking. Passing to the left side of the doorway, we notice the vanquished Serpent is descending head downwards; while Good and Evil contend, in the form of a lion and a dragon, upon the capital, the pillar beneath being enriched with two figures bearing the Cross of the Church and the Sword of State. Over the entrance springs the Tree of Life, bearing goodly fruit, and round about may be traced various fowls of the air, in more or less mythical forms.

Upon entering the church, we are at once impressed by the quiet dignity of this massive style of building; with its subdued touches o enrichment upon the carved pillars on each side of the arch which separates nave from chancel, representing the four Evangelists; and in the bold *zigzag* ornament on the arch above. It is wonderful what an effect of length is obtained, in so small a building, by the double series of arches and the semicircular apse at the end; and how Nature, abhorring a blank space, has painted the old walls in varying tones of mellow colours, which, however, are viewed askance by the caretaker, who, holding to the opinion that 'cleanliness is next to godliness,' will not be satisfied until the weather-stained carvings appear resplendent in a fresh coat of whitewash.

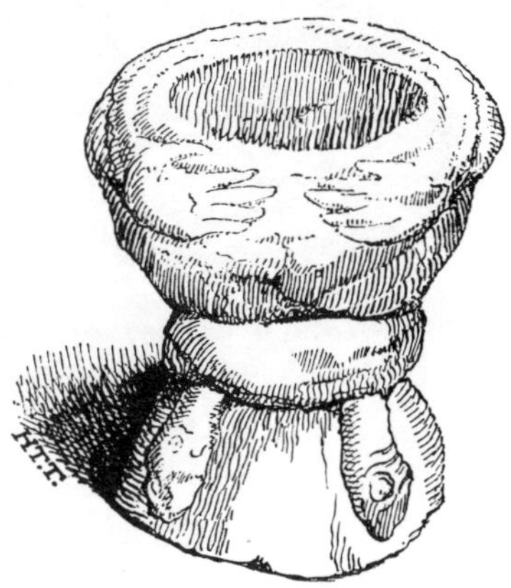

SAXON FONT, KILPECK.

The large old font of conglomerate stone, which figures so prominently in our sketch of the interior, is still in use, having superseded a venerable Saxon one of curious form, which now stands in the apse.

Outside the church a series of grotesquely-carved heads, some seventy in number, runs around the building; terminated at the west end by a pair of peculiar monsters, with vast jaws and curling tongues, which have a very strange appearance.

After a short run by train we disembark at Pontrilas, 'quite a place,' as our American cousins say, in its position as a railway junction, and convenient as a centre whence to survey this beautiful

south-western corner of the shire. Hither, then, we will retrace our steps after we have explored the country 'served' by that most eccentric of lines, the Golden Valley Railway; where we have seen *the* linesman, when not engaged in haymaking on the railway-bank, deeply engrossed over his occupation of weeding between the rails, as we waited for the train which, if we are to believe the tongue of rumour, sometimes fails to put in an appearance, the company's only locomotive having been seized for distraint of rent.

Here at Pontrilas occurred the first local encounter between the rival parties during the Civil Wars, when, in a skirmish between Royalist and Roundhead troops, the first blood was shed in this county.

Those who are endowed with a good stock of patience may avail themselves of the above-mentioned railway route, to visit the noble abbey church of Dore ; but we prefer, this bright sunny morning, a trudge past Pontrilas Court, a picturesque stone mansion of the days of the maiden queen, at one time an inn much frequented by lovers of 'the gentle art,' but in these latter days the residence of St. J. Attwood Mathews, Esq., the present high sheriff of the county.

Pursuing our way across the meadows, we pass through Ewias Harold, a pretty village whose trim cottages, bowered in climbing plants, are grouped in a nonchalant way around the massive tower of the well-cared-for church; and thence we climb the breezy, gorse-clad common, which affords such lovely views of villages nestling in the secluded vale, encompassed by noble ranges of hills ; conspicuous among them the lonely double peak of the Skyrrid or Holy Mountain—a Matterhorn *in petto*—and the flat-topped Sugarloaf near 'Abergenny :' Graig and Garway hills raise their broad shoulders above the woods of Kentchurch Park, and to the westward the abrupt heights of Hatterel Hill bound the vista with many a mile of wild, fern-clad moorland, overtopping the grass-grown slopes of Mynydd Ferddin, where the Welsh tradition has it that Merlin lies buried. This wide prospect, overarched by a breezy sky flecking the distant landscape with ever-changing effects, affords a store of unalloyed pleasure to carry away in our memory—a rose without a thorn.

This charming neighbourhood is, thanks to its secluded situation and absence of accommodation for visitors, almost a *terra incognita* to the generality of holiday-folk ; and has consequently preserved its natural beauties to a far greater degree than in more frequented districts.

Glancing across the vale, we mark the tree-begirt knoll where formerly stood a castle, once the head of a great lordship, whose founder gave his name to the place. 'The fame goeth,' says Leland, 'that Kynge Harold had a son namyd Harold, and of this Harold part

EWIAS HAROLD CHURCH.

of Ewis was namyd Ewis Harold. The fame is that the castell of Map-Herald was buildid of Harold, afore he was Kynge, and when he overcam the Walsche-men, Harold gave this castell to his son.'

A cell of Black monks once existed here which, Leland tells us, 'was translatyd from Dulesse village, a myle and upper on the broke. Dulesse village longed to Harold; Filius Haraldi foundyd this at Dulesse; Robertus Tregoz translatyd it from Dulesse to Map-Heralt; it was a cell to Gloucester.' This castle of Harold's formed a link in the chain of strongholds, which once guarded this frontier land on the Welsh border, from Clifford on the Wye, through Snodhill and Ewias Harold to Grosmont and Skenfrith, the latter near the house of the Knights Templars at Garway; with outworks at Longtown and Old Castle. Indeed, the face of this fair country is closely besprinkled with camps and castles of antique construction, bearing witness to long-continued struggles in bygone times for the possession of these much coveted march-lands.

From certain hints received, we decide to made a détour, in order to examine the little church at Rowlstone. A secluded and grass-grown lane, which we follow from Ewias Harold, is of quite a Welsh character; the road gradually ascending, and becoming about as steep as they make them, even in these hilly parts of the country. A solitary woman, leaning on a hoe, who informs us that she is 'widdocking the whit' (weeding the wheat), appears the sole inhabitant of the district; until we descend suddenly upon the little hamlet, and the church we are in search of.

STONE-CARVING, ROWLSTONE CHURCH.

Dedicated to St. Peter, the tiny edifice bears, in many of its details, quaint references to its patron saint, whose effigy we observe represented head downwards upon the wall, with devices of cocks in a string course running around the chancel arch; the same pointed reference to its patronymic occurring in the two curious old candle-brackets, unique of their kind, on the side-walls of the chancel. As shown in our sketch, these remarkable pieces of fourteenth-century ironwork are arranged, each to bear five long candles upon the 'prickets' on the lower bar, passing through the rings above; the brackets being ornamented with cocks and fleurs-de-lis, and hinged to fold back against the wall. The church possesses an unusual treasure in a well-preserved black-letter Welsh Bible, wherein, on the title-page of the New Testament, we read that this is 'Testament Newydd, ein Harglwydd Jesu Grist, anno 1588.'

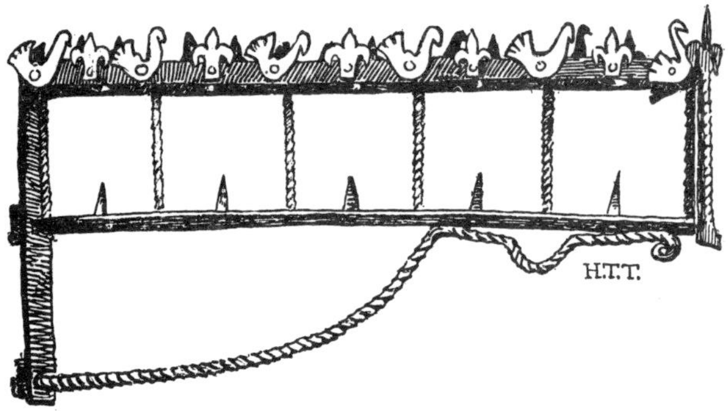

CANDLE-BRACKET, ROWLSTONE CHURCH.

Pondering these things over a ruminative pipe, we retrace our steps—downhill, this time—to Ewias Harold; and push forward over the common, now green with waving bracken, amidst which the sheep and donkeys of the humble cottars are almost lost to sight. This is a notable scene in autumn, when the glory of the gorse-bloom is upon it, glowing golden against the purple background of the distance.

A rough, rambling track takes us steeply down by the shortest route to the village of Dore; the tower of its ancient abbey church giving us our direction as we descend.

Pausing to lean on the stile by the churchyard wall, let us glance back at the interesting past history of this noble building; still impressive from its venerable traditions, and stately even in its present diminished proportions.

The name of Dore has been the cause of much weighty conjecture; but common-sense suggests that, when the Normans came into the district, and found the stream which runs through the valley passing under the generic British name 'Dwr,' they transformed the original name into the—to their ears—familiar form of 'Val d'Or,' the 'Vallis Aurea' of the old monks of Dore; nowadays *anglicé* Golden Valley.

That close observer Leland, thus quaintly describes the situation of the abbey: 'The broke Dour runneth by the Abbay of Dour; and there it breakethe, a little above the monasterie, into two armes; whereof the lesse arme runnethe throwghe the monasterie; the bigger arme levith the Abbay a bowe-shot of on the right hond, or banke; the confluence is againe hard bynethe the Abbay.' This minute account holds good to the present day; the clear stream, well stocked with many a 'lusty trout,' prattles through the rich meadow-lands 'hard bynethe' the ancient walls; and serves, as of yore, to turn the wheel of the mill erected by the provident monks.

The abbey of Dore was originally the home of a community of Cistercian monks, and is, so far as we know, the only instance of a church of that fraternity now remaining in use in this country.

Of the magnificent church founded in the twelfth century by Robert de Ewyas, the transepts, choir and chapels alone remain; but these are of such goodly size as to show that, when complete, the building must have been of truly noble proportions: beautiful still are the details of its carving and ornamentation, and in such perfect state as to show how the early sculptor felt his way, from the harsh lines of Norman work, towards the lovely foliage which developed into perfection during the thirteenth century. To quote Mr. Blashill, who has given close attention to the building; 'Some of these capitals, which are 700 years old, are, I think, unmatched in style and workmanship by anything done either then or since.'

In Henry VIII.'s reign, the great abbey with its offices, chapter-house and cloisters, was demolished, and its materials sold, and the demesne granted to John Scudamore of Holme Lacy; after which liberal confiscation the plunderers were pleased to appoint a certain John

Phelyps to the cure of souls at Dore, for the sum of fifty shillings, paid *yearly*, under the style of 'wages.' It is, therefore, not surprising to find the church falling into neglect, so that it was afterwards in great part dismantled; but service was still conducted, under difficulties, by one John Giles, who used to come on the Sunday to read prayers in the forlorn ruins, standing, as we read, under the shelter of an arch to keep his book from the wet.

In this deplorable state did the abbey continue for about a century,

until restored to use by the munificence of the then Lord Scudamore, who upon one occasion gave a purse of gold at the offertory, with the contents of which the present communion-plate was purchased.

To this noble benefactor is attributed the erection of the tower, the re-roofing of the church, and the massive screen enclosing the chancel, surmounted by three large shields bearing, respectively, the arms of England, of Scudamore, and of the See of Hereford ; beneath which runs the following motto: 'Vivere Deo gratus: Toti mundo tumulatus: Crimine mundatus: Semper transire paratus.' In the construction of these important works, Viscount Scudamore called to his aid that invaluable carpenter, John Abell; and it may be noted, *en passant,* that the inscription above quoted is identical with the words previously transcribed from Abell's market-house at Leominster.

SEAL OF DORE ABBEY.

In early times, the abbey church received numerous endowments; King John, in the last year of his reign, presenting to the monastery 'all the land between the River Dore and the rivulet called Trivelbrook;' a gift that had been first plundered, then bestowed, and lastly consecrated to God by a king who was a confirmed law-breaker. In the middle of the thirteenth century we find Acquablanca, Bishop of Hereford, granting release of penance to all persons who contribute to the beautifying of 'the sumptuous church of Dore;' which was consecrated by his successor, Saint Thomas Cantilupe, who conducted the ceremony at considerable personal risk from the armed Welsh partisans of the Bishop of Menevia (St. David's), who claimed this as part of his diocese.

By the pleasant arrangement of the present rector, the Rev. A. Phillipps, the gates of the great porch stand always unlocked; a somewhat rare custom, worthy of imitation. Descending a few steps we enter the south transept, when the lofty and well-proportioned arches of the 'crossing' at once impress the eye, although this part of the church, having been covered with a thick coat of whitewash at some past time, has a rather bare appearance.

To our right is the chapel of the Hoskyns family, whose estates were, 'once upon a time,' so extensive that it was commonly said, the master could ride across his own land all the way from Harewood to Bacton, a distance of about ten miles. It was at Morehampton Court, in this parish, that Serjeant Hoskyns entertained King James I. with a morris-dance by five old couples, whose combined ages amounted to a thousand years.

High up in the wall of the north transept may be discerned the doorway by which the brethren entered the church from their own apartments; and on the floor beneath, our attention is called to the date cut upon the tombstone of Elizabeth Lewis, who died in 1715 at the respectable age, as would appear at the first glance, of 141 years; but upon closer inspection it may be seen that some facetious wight has 'improved the shining hour' by inserting the two 'ones' alongside the original 'four.'

This part of the church, although no longer in use, retains the carved-oak box pews and gallery put up in the seventeenth century, and a few rude frescoes upon the bare walls.

The beautiful chancel only is used for service, having been screened in for that purpose by the rector; thus forming a compact little church, well adapted to the wants of the small congregation. The altar-table is composed of a single slab of stone 12 feet long, which, after lying buried for many years, was unearthed and put to the ignominious use of salting meat and making cheese upon; but is now restored to its original place and purpose, supported on short, massive pillars. A series of finely-moulded windows above are filled with stained glass, in one of which we espy the date 1634, that of the restoration of the church.

But it is not until we have passed round by the aisle, that the distinguishing feature of this noble church discloses itself, in the exquisite series of vaulted chapels, supported upon groups of clustered pillars, the capitals of which are carved with beautifully-designed foliage, each one differing from its neighbour. The slender columns show signs of colouring beneath the all-pervading coating of whitewash of the 'churchwarden' era, which somewhat detracts from the sharpness of the detail in the carver's work. In the recess of a window lies a small stone effigy, which has been the subject of much conjecture; this is supposed to have marked the burial-place of the heart of John Le Breton, a Bishop of Hereford. Camden avers that Dore was a place where many of the nobility and gentry of these parts were interred,

DORE ABBEY.

and that Walter de Plokenet, Ganfrid de Geneville, and William and Roger de Clifford, found their last resting-places here.

Many traces remain, showing that the abbey precincts once spread afar over meadows where nowadays flocks are feeding; here and there in cottage garden-walls, the very stones cry out against the vandalism which has utilized, in their construction, the plinths, arches and corbels of the ancient fabric. The monks of old built granaries which, if they no longer can boast a 'local habitation,' still retain 'a name' at such places as Hollen Grange, New Barns, and Morehampton Grange in the vicinity; the abbots deriving considerable revenues from the produce of the fat demesne lands, which were appropriated to the purposes of the establishment.

Let us now pass out through the quiet churchyard, where the hot sun of a summer noontide is flecked by the shade of many an over-arching tree. Following up the vale of little Dore stream we find, hard by its course, a mill-leat passing to the 'over-shot' mill at New Court. This is but a sorry relic of certain works of irrigation, carried out on an ambitious scale by Rowland Vaughan, a worthy scion of the ancient house of the 'Vaughans of Bredwardine;' the author of a rare and curious book, published in the sixteenth century, entitled 'Most approved and long experienced Water Works.'

The intention of this singularly practical and sensible, although speculative, work was to establish a commonwealth of labour in this 'happy valley.' 'The Golden Vale,' says Vaughan, 'the Lombardy of Herefordshire, the Garden of the old gallants, is the Paradise of all the parts beyond the Severn. I propose to raise a Golden Worlde in the Golden Valley, being the pride of all that countree bordering on Wales, joyning on Ewyas Lacy; the richest, yet for want of employment, the plentyfullest place of Poore in the Kingdome. There bee, within a mile and a halfe from my House, every way, five hundred poore Habitations, whose greatest meanes consist in spinning flax, hemps, and Hurdes.'

There was to be a parson 'for the salvation of the soule, lest all my buildings and foundations be shattle and sandy.' Vaughan gives a curious account of his choice of a preacher for his new colony: 'There came unto me,' he says, 'a young minister, having a good witte, a good memory, and a pretty dribble of learning; who made himselfe fitte to teach children: who, however, had no sooner received the benefit of this benefice, but the principall of his Parishioners told me I had planted a Machiavel among them, a cunning usurer.' We can hardly be surprised at his difficulty in finding a suitable pastor, when we learn that, about this time, a young preacher in the same district 'has ten poundes in money, to make eight quarter sermons yearly; which preacher ventures his life sixteen times over the great River Wye, and as many more up and down a huge Hill lying in his way.'

Of Rowland Vaughan's early attempts to establish a commercial Utopia in this remote region, a few traces are still extant, in the channels or ducts and other appliances near the river Dore—mute witnesses to the skill and ingenuity of a man whose ideas were far in advance of his time, smacking not a little of the cult of the latter-day socialist.

Up at Bacton Church, whose ivy-mantled tower is seen on the hill above Dore, lies buried 'that honourable and virtuous Gentlewoman' Mistress Blanche Parry, of New Court in this parish; the life-long companion and faithful maid-of-honour to Queen Elizabeth. Her handsome monument stands in the chancel, having the two figures of Mistress Parry and her Queen, in the characteristic gowns and ruffs of their day; in a kneeling position, beneath a classic canopy, bearing the arms of the family and a tablet, whereon is inscribed in antique lettering a curious legend, of which the following is a literal copy:

'I Parryehys dovghter Blaenche, of Newe Covrte borne,
That traenyd was in pryncys' courts, wythe gorgiovs wyghts
Wheare fleetynge honor sounds wythe blaste of horne;
Each of accovnte too place of worldes delyghts,
Am lodgyd heere wythe in thys stonye toombe,
My harpynger ys paede, I owght of due,
My frynds of speeche heere in doo fynde mee doombe.
The whiche in vaene they doo so greatlye rhve:
For so mooche as hyt ys but thende of all.
Thys wordlye rowte of State, what so they be:

BLANCHE PARRY'S MONUMENT, BACTON.

The whiche untoo the reste heerafter shall
  Assemble thvs each wyghte in hys degree.
I lyvde allwys as handmaede too a Quene;
  In chamber chiff, my tyme dyd tooverpasse;
Uncarefull of my wellthe ther was I sene,
  Whyllste I abode the ronnynge of my glasse;
Not dovbtynge wante, whyllste that my mystres lyvde,
  In womans state, whose cradell sawe I rockte:
Her servaunte then, as when shee her crowne attcheeved;
  And so remaend, tyll deathe my doore had knockte;
Preferrynge styll the causye of eache wyghte,
  As farre as I doorste move her Grace hys eare,
For too rewarde decerts, by course of ryghte;
  As needs resulte of sarvys doone eache weare;
So that my tyme I thus dyd passe awaye,
  A maede in courte and never no man's wyffe;
Sworne of Quene Ellsbeth's hedd chamber allwaye,
  Wythe maeden Quene, a maede dyd ende my lyffe.'

There were formerly in Bacton Church some fine painted windows, memorials of Milo ap Parry, grandfather of Blanche; but these were unfortunately removed early in the present century, and set up in Atcham Church, Salop.

At the time of our visit there is no incumbent living at Bacton, so the few treasures belonging to the church are in the safe-keeping of a resident in the locality; to whose courtesy we are indebted for the opportunity to examine the curious piece of embroidery, worked by the fair hand of Blanche Parry, which did duty at one time as an altar-cloth here. That it was not originally intended for this purpose may be seen from the way in which various pieces are joined together; it is very probable that they are portions of a Court gown, of the time of Queen Elizabeth: the quaint devices representing frogs, snails, deer, caterpillars, dogs, etc., amidst foliage, are worked on cloth of silver, in a very realistic manner, the colours being well preserved, with the exception of the gold thread which, in the lapse of years, has become somewhat tarnished.

The beautiful little silver-gilt chalice belonging to the church, probably owes its preservation from the hand of the iconoclast to the remote situation of this parish, whither it is supposed to have been brought from Llanthony Priory, in Monmouthshire. This elegant little vessel is, with the exception of a beautiful one at Leominster, the only specimen of an ancient chalice remaining in this county. It was probably made about the year 1500, and is inscribed with the name of the donor, John Capull; one of the spandrels of the base is engraved with a figure, supposed to represent our Saviour, the hands being raised above the head. The ancient paten, also treasured here, is ornamented with a head chased upon its centre.

CHALICE AT BACTON.

Farewell now to Bacton; for we must away to 'fresh woods and pastures new,' awaiting us within the compass of the Golden Valley. An hour's stroll across the meadows takes the wayfarer to the twin parishes of Turnaston and Vowchurch, the latter having a station upon the before-mentioned railway. Anent these two curious names, a piece of derivation is offered for what it is worth: Tradition says that, some few centuries—more or less—ago, two pious maiden ladies resolved to build a church which should be available for both parishes; but, disagreeing upon the question of a site for the edifice, they fell to words, the elder lady exclaiming, 'I *Vow* I will build my *church,* before you *Turn a stone* of yours!' And there stand the twin churches to this day, a bow-shot distance asunder. Vowchurch is noticeable from the peculiar arrangement of massive oak supports, black with age, which rise from the floor to the roof; this is, we believe, an almost unique feature: the rival church at Turnaston has a pretty timber porch, and contains an alabaster slab, with a recumbent figure of a knight, and black-letter inscription of the sixteenth century.

In the Rolls of Swinfield, Bishop of Hereford, it is recorded that 'at Turnaston, in the Golden Vale, in 1298, an armed band, instigated by Hugh Devereux and Richard Dansey, took forcible possession of the church, and chapel of St. Leonard, and the houses of the incumbents. The Bishop entreated King Edward I. to command the Sheriff to remove them, so that the ministers might exercise their offices in peace.'

White House, situated in this parish, the home of the ancient family of the Howorths, contains some interesting paintings and portraits, and stands amidst beautiful hanging woods. At Michaelchurch Court, a couple of miles to the rear, are some fine examples of wood-carving and panelling; while, hidden away in the adjoining vale of the infant Monnow, in a secluded spot beneath the shadow of the Black Mountains, stand the scanty remains of Crasswall Abbey, a small priory founded here in the reign of King John, which was subordinate to the Order of Grandmont in Normandy, and was supported by a prior and ten monks. The primitive little parish church, no great distance away, has upon its northern side the cock-pit where, in the 'good old days,' the men of the congregation were wont to relieve their pent-up feelings, after the constraint of morning service, by enjoying a set-to with a 'main' of cocks!

But to return to our 'Happy Valley.' Having seen the wonders of Vowchurch and Turnaston, we journey on to the larger village of Peterchurch, which may be called the capital of the valley. The church, whose tall spire 'heaven-directed, and pointing to the sky,' forms a conspicuous landmark far and wide, is a most interesting example of the Norman style. The chancel is built in an apsidal form, and on the south wall of the nave is a stone tablet built in, on which is portrayed a fish with a gold chain round its neck, from which is suspended a gold ring: this may be taken to represent either a miraculous trout, caught in St. Peter's Well, hard by; or as a reference to the miraculous draught of fishes.

In an out-of-the-way position among the hills to the westward stands Uris-hay Castle, perched upon a height commanding a wide prospect over hill and dale. Originally granted by William the Conqueror to a Baron De-la-Haye, the owner of the castle has to this day, through all the chances and changes of time, borne the name of Delahay. Adjoining the house are the remains of a building which has been, within sixty years, a church, a dissenting chapel, a carpenter's shop, a dog-kennel and a lumber-room—'facile descensus Averni.'

Between Peterchurch and the next station at Dorstone, the hill upon which stands the Castle of Snodhill is a prominent object, projecting into the valley and commanding the road towards Hay. The ruins indicate that this fortress was built at various periods: William the Norman bestowed it on Hugh de l'Aisme, and in the reign of Stephen it was counted among the 1,200 castles in the land. In the fourteenth century, Robert Chandos held it by barony and service of knight; and later it was held by a member of that family against the onslaught of Owen Glendower, who took up his position at a place still bearing the name of Dragon's Pool; he having assumed the title of 'The Dragon,' in emulation of the famous Uther Pendragon.

Elizabeth granted Snodhill Castle to her favourite, Dudley Earl of Leicester—about which time it is described by Leland as 'somewhat in ruines'; and, as we find that Lord Leicester disposed of the castle after the short interval of four months, we may infer that the gift was rather to enable her favourite to raise funds, than to enjoy as a possession.

The fine old seventeenth-century court-house near by, a good specimen of the country mansion of that period, retains some massive oak beams and panelled chambers, although fallen somewhat into decay.

Extending our ramble through Dorstone village, we climb the hill before us by the side of an ancient and overgrown trackway, running steeply up between the fields, and overshadowed by sombre old yew-trees. Hence a field-path leads to the broad, level top of the ridge where, beside an old grass-grown lane, stands a monument before whose antiquity the relics of Roman and Saxon days seem but things of yesterday. To trace the history of the great cromlech called 'Arthur's Stone' leads one back into the mists of a prehistoric era, when the mystic rites of the Druids were enacted, amidst the silent solitudes of this bleak hill-top; in full view of the sharp-peaked Skyrrid, or Holy Mountain, which is conspicuous due south. The altar-stone, though years ago robbed of a great piece for road-mending, is still some twenty feet in length, and its huge bulk inevitably suggests the unanswerable enigma: How did those men of old raise such ponderous masses from their resting-places on Mother Earth?

Many a changing scene has this old cromlech witnessed, since the worship of the primæval god Thor gave to it the name of 'Thor-stein.'

ARTHUR'S STONE.

Bridging over in imagination the events of earlier ages, we come down to the year 1645, when, one September day, King Charles I., in the course of his wanderings, awaited beside the cromlech a portion of his Scottish cavalry, crossing the Wye from Byford; who, in sad and sorry plight, were set upon and worried by dogs at a place below the hill, still bearing the name of 'Scotland Bank.'

After pausing to sketch this patriarch among monuments, we may take a stretch along the old British road across the open hillside to Murbage Point, whence we can promise our reader, should the day be clear, as it was our fortune to have it, one of the very finest panoramas in all this land of fair prospects.

Or we may descend from the cromlech by a footpath, passing beneath the giant oaks amidst the glades of Moccas Park. Moccas Court, the residence of the Rev. Sir G. Cornewall, Bart.—whose family trace their descent from Richard, Earl of Poictiers, one of the sons of King John—is said to be partly constructed from the ruins of Bredwardine Castle, a place of considerable size and importance in the time of the Vaughans. Be that as it may, its situation is most happily chosen, the grounds exhibiting the rare botanical taste of Sir George, who has here collected, among many other curiosities, examples of all the handsomest of native wild plants. Verdant lawns slope hence to a broad reach of the Wye, terminated by the rugged sandstone cliffs of Brobury Scar, impending above one of the most picturesque bends of the river. Adjacent to the mansion lies the curious little Norman Church, perhaps the oldest in the county, adorned with a carved tympanum over the door, symbolical of the Tree of Life; and many other interesting features. Hence a noble avenue of old Scotch firs, known as 'Monnington Walk,' leads to the village of that name, the traditional burial-place of Owen Glendower, leader of the last 'invasion' of England.

Returning to Dorstone, we there rejoin the Lilliputian train, and thus, in leisurely wise, retrace our steps to our starting-point at Pontrilas; whence we proceed upon further voyages of discovery in other directions.

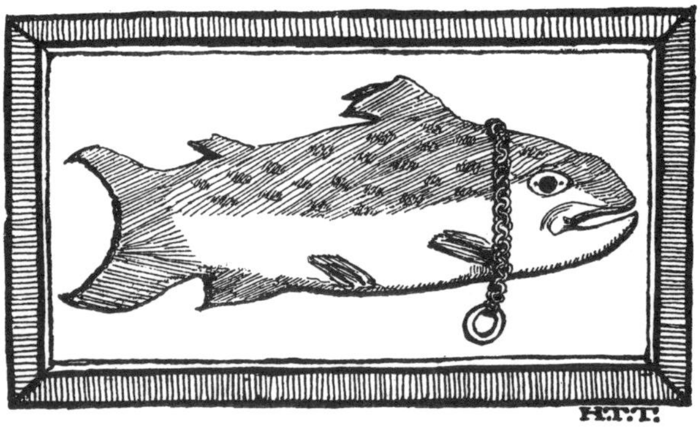

PANEL AT PETERCHURCH.

A RAMBLE FROM PONTRILAS TO ROSS.

TURNING up a road by a farm-house near Pontrilas Court, an ancient home of the Baskervilles, we enter upon a district known in olden times as Gwent, 'the Fair Land;' a name which lingers in the district, and, in a slightly changed form, survives in such names as Kentchurch, Kenderchurch, and others.

As we advance the prospect widens, extending across the Vale of Monnow to Grosmont, a decayed old town, formerly governed by a mayor, burgesses, and an ale-taster! The famous trout-stream is spanned just here by a bridge, built to replace a more ancient one; the origin of this latter is the subject of the following quaint local legend, which is still an article of faith among the old folk of the country-side. His Satanic majesty was pleased, so the story goes, to enter into a compact with a certain learned divine of the neighbourhood, named John of Kent, to build a bridge across the Monnow, bringing stones for the purpose from Garway Hill; and the spot is still pointed out in which the devil, upon hearing the cock crow, let fall some rocks from his apron. All that the builders constructed during the night fell down each ensuing day; but at length the bridge was completed, and the Evil One stipulated that he must have the first passenger for himself. Howbeit, the astute priest stole a march upon his crafty comrade, by rolling a loaf of bread upon the bridge, and so enticing a dog across.

Down in the valley, just across the Welsh border, we espy that once notorious hostelry, the 'Monmouth Cap' of coaching days—a sign deriving its origin from that article of headgear referred to by Fluellen in 'Henry V.' at the battle of Agincourt, where he speaks of

KENTCHURCH COURT.

his countrymen 'wearing leeks in their Monmouth caps'; and they are also mentioned, among other gifts presented to Lord Gilbert Talbot of Goodrich, as 'a new Yeare's Gifte of a Monmouth Cappe.'

At the turnpike we choose the broad walk, shaded by a fine avenue of forest trees, in preference to the 'hard highroad.' Before us the noble front of Garway Hill rises above the finely-timbered park, sheltering the stately home of that ancient and honourable family the Scudamores—a name which, derived from their motto 'Scutum amoris Divini,' so frequently occurs in connection with leading events during the past history of the county.

Though pleasantly situated, the castellated mansion at Kentchurch stands in a position which does not afford any particular view, being surrounded by trees: the earliest portion is the lofty stone building called Owen Glendower's Tower, of Henry IV.'s time, which is surmounted by a curiously contorted stack of chimneys.

Here, in the fourteenth century, lived John of Kent—or 'Jacky Kent,' as he is styled throughout the countryside—of whom a curious old portrait, painted on a panel, is preserved in the mansion. Being a member of the Protestant sect of the Lollards, and private chaplain to Lord Scudamore, this remarkable man acquired knowledge beyond the comprehension of his neighbours, among whom he was commonly reputed to have made a compact with the devil, with whom, as we have seen, he appears to have been on intimate terms; who granted him extraordinary gifts in return for the possession of his body and soul; threatening John that he would have him, when he died, whether he were buried 'in church or out of it;' this, however, the learned man cleverly evaded by causing his body to be interred beneath the wall, half within and half without the church.

A cellar is still shown which, according to tradition, John of Kent used as a stable, wherein he kept a swift horse ready saddled to enable him to fly with lightning speed at a moment's notice.

But, to return from the region of myths, let us take a peep at the comely church nestling, with its pretty vicarage-house, close on the borders of the park. The interior contains fine recumbent marble figures, in good preservation, of a Scudamore and his wife and children; very finely cut, and retaining much of the original colouring.

We now wend our way through the spacious and finely-wooded park, some four miles around, which climbs the steep shoulder of Garway Hill. Beneath the great oaks the deer are sheltering in groups;

and here we observe that, although the foliage of the yew-tree is generally injurious to animals, the *dead* leaves of that tree are eaten without causing any ill effect. A curious provision of nature among the horned deer is the fact that, at a certain season of the year when the horns are shed, the animals are in the habit of devouring them, in order to increase their stock of carbonate of lime, to aid in the building-up of new antlers.

Passing from the park near an old quarry, we enter a pretty country road, closely following the course of the Monnow, which here flows through a narrow valley beneath the twin heights of Graig and Garway; a farmhouse high on the hill above bears the suggestive title of Cold Nose, while the names of White House and Black House are dotted all over the map hereabouts.

Steeply climbs the road across the brow of the hill, the peewits piping plaintively, and sweeping in circles across the path of the unwonted intruder. A sudden turn reveals the massive old tower of Garway Church, in a hollow beside the road. Here was, in olden times, a famous preceptory of those monastic soldiers, the Knights Templars, to whom Henry II. granted all his estate of 'Llan Garway.' At a later period their successors, the Knights Hospitallers, took over this establishment; and built the interesting columbarium which stands, neglected, amidst the modern farm-buildings, a barely-decipherable inscription over the doorway running as follows: 'In the year

1326 this Dove-cot was built by Brother Richard.' The interior is provided with 666 pigeon-holes, is domed over with a stone vault, and bears, cut upon the stonework (in reference probably to its past history), a recumbent cross of the Knights Templars, with an upright cross of the Hospitallers.

Silas Taylor, in the days of the Protectorate, tells us that, in his time, 'There were stately Ruines of a religious House at Garway': but these have now entirely disappeared.

The time-worn edifice close at hand is a perfect example of an early border church; its massive, solidly-built tower standing at a curious angle to the nave, with which it is connected by a short passage, in such a manner as to render it capable of defence against the incursions of Welsh marauders, no infrequent occurrence in these wild districts in mediæval times. The chancel is separated from the nave by an uncommonly fine Norman arch, of peculiar construction, and rather Saracenic in appearance; close beside it are the steps which led to the rood-loft. The huge old benches, rudely but strongly made of oak some five inches in thickness, would cause the modern 'stained and varnished' style of work to look somewhat shame-faced; indeed, throughout the whole church, there is a rude vigour of character that is enhanced by the weather-stained aspect of the sacred edifice, recalling the words of Crabbe:

> 'See how Nature's work is done,
> How slowly true she lays her colours on;
> When her least speck, upon the hardest flint,
> Has mark and form, and is a living tint.'

We now descend to the quaint little village of Skenfrith, which lies at our feet in a sheltered nook, beside the pretty Monnow stream; some of the cottages here lean sociably against the outer walls of the ruined castle, within which the thrifty villagers have reared a thriving orchard.

At the farther end of the hamlet the church raises its picturesque timbered bell-turret above the lowly dwellings; the unrestored interior contains some boldly carved box-pews, and a handsome stone table-monument, carved with very characteristic figures, representing a sixteenth-century knight, named Morgan, and his family: the last occupant of this castle, and commander of the neighbouring border strongholds at Grosmont and White Castle.

Crossing the bridge, we ascend steeply by the old coach-road, past a large deserted inn to Broad Oak; whence we diverge to the right, to get a peep at the ruins of Pembridge Castle, of which considerable portions of ivy-clad outer walls and gateway remain, converted to the purpose of a farm-house.

Perhaps the most remarkable point about the place is the striking view, from its elevated situation, of the lofty mountain summits to the westward, separating the Valley of the Wye from that of the Usk—a group of graceful peaks, which form a charming contrast to the rich woodlands in the valley far beneath.

At a place called The Cwm, in the adjoining parish of Llanrothal, was formerly a Jesuit college, which was dispersed by Bishop Croft, by order of Parliament, in the year 1678, when the books appertaining to it were taken to the library of Hereford Cathedral. A very curious pamphlet relating to the college, which was published at the time, is now in the safe custody of an appreciative resident in that city.

Perched upon a conspicuous knoll, away in the distance, the solid tower of St. Weonard's Church shall be our guide-mark; a route which leads us through ripening cornfields, whose pale gold is shot with the brilliant scarlet of innumerable poppies. Out from beneath our very feet springs a covey of partridges, blustering off on noisy wings. The lowly blossoms of the 'shepherd's weather-glass,' clustering closely upon the red-brown earth, tell a flattering tale, with wide-open petals, this hot summer day; the hedgerows, too, are veiled with broad mantles of the beautiful 'traveller's joy,' and the hazels show clusters of fast-ripening nuts in many a tangled brake.

A glance at any one of the numerous sign-posts in our line of march tells us, by the unmistakably Celtic character of the place-names, that we are on the Welsh side of the Wye; for this is the broad and fertile land of Archenfield, the 'Ergyng' of olden times, when it was governed by its own independent kinglet, and was, in Henry VIII.'s time, already famed for the quality of its wool; when we read of a certain John Lloyd undertaking, in 1511, to deliver to Hereford 'wool of the best veynes within Irchinfield.'

Passing by a group of bowery cottages beside a stream at 'Little London,' and breasting the steep slope of Hunger Hill, which this hot afternoon one is disposed to rechristen 'Thirsty Hill,' we see on ahead the group of Scotch firs which adorns the summit of a huge old 'tump,' the burial-place, presumably, of some ancient ruler in Archenfield, and until recent years the chosen spot for the morris-dances of the villagers.

Skirting the base of the venerable mound, we enter the church, which contains a huge old chest, carved out of a solid oaken baulk, and bound with iron bands: in the Mynors' chapel, enclosed within an open screen, is the pew assigned to the family of that name, whose coat-of-arms is suspended from the wall, which is also ornamented with a quaintly-conceived panel of wood-carving, representing Abraham preparing for the sacrifice of his son Isaac.

Turning down a steep lane, we now make for Treago, the venerable home of the Mynors, catching picturesque glimpses of the mansion through the embowering trees as we approach.

Treago is almost unique as a fortified dwelling-house of the thirteenth century, which has been in the possession of the same family ever since it was built—a fortune which few mansions in this country, of anything like similar antiquity, can boast. This appears to have been the original seat of the Mynors, who also had possessions at Burghill in this county, and elsewhere.

John de Miners was appointed by Edward II. keeper of St. Briavel's Castle, and of the Forest of Dean, and from him the family trace a direct descent till the year 1765, when the estate passed to a descendant named Peter Rickards, who assumed the name of Mynors; to whose heirs the property still appertains. This ancient family, settled so long in Treago, has, in the natural order of things, contracted alliances with most of the great border families, among whom is included the great house of Baskerville.

The noble old fortified dwelling-house remains, in its intrinsic features, as originally built, with massive stone walls some seven feet in thickness, having a circular tower at each angle; enclosing a court-yard which has been built over to meet modern requirements. The great south-eastern tower, which was larger than the others, had a flight of stone stairs, and contained the kitchens, whose position is indicated by the bulge in the wall, caused by an oven near the present entrance-door, seen in our view. The projecting story above is the handiwork of a later occupant, who had a fancy to retire to this lofty eerie to contemplate the landscape, or smoke the soothing weed. The ancient hall, which has been converted into a kitchen, had an open timber roof, much resembling that of Westminster Hall.

The small windows giving light into the tourelles were strongly

TREAGO.

barred, even the window of 'The Ladyes' Chamber,' though of somewhat larger dimensions, being protected in the same manner. The œillets which commanded the side next the hill, being the weakest point of the defence, had a projecting stone beneath each, on the inside, for the use of the archer in discharging his missiles. In Henry VIII.'s time the great entrance gateway was added; a solid, massive piece of masonry, with bold Tudor archway.

A ramble through the interior leads us along tortuous passages, up and down steps in unexpected corners, and into sundry secret chambers; one of which, having been used to secrete a Romish priest during Reformation days, is known as the 'Pope's hole.' Upon the walls of the hall hang various portraits of the Mynors of former times, one fair scion being pointed out as having been instrumental in saving the house, at some critical period during the 'brave days of old.'

The moat which surrounded the mansion has been replaced by a modern terrace and carriage-drive, and the inevitable tennis-lawn; but all these concomitants of nineteenth-century life are so arranged that they in no wise detract from the time-honoured appearance of the mansion.

Returning to St. Weonards, a path leads through the wheat-fields to the tiny hamlet of Tretire, beyond which, at the parting of the coach-roads, stand St. Owen's Cross, where, in mediæval times, the priest was wont to address the countryfolks on their way to Hentland church.

From St. Owen's Cross we take the left-hand road for half a mile, passing over the site of some long-forgotten battle at a place still called Camp Field: hence a cart-track, which strikes off to the left, brings us in a few minutes to the ancient moated farm-house known as Gillow.

This curious fortified manor-house is situated, after the mediæval custom, in a secluded dell, in such a manner that a passing enemy might easily overlook its existence. We enter the building by a bridge across the moat, through a Tudor arch beneath the massive, battlemented tower; a small courtyard gives access to the dwelling-house, which occupies three sides of the square. The interior shows evidences of earlier buildings; a good traceried window, now partly blocked up, gave light into a chapel dedicated to St. David, which has now degenerated to the uses of a dairy. In the basement a curious stone effigy, apparently of a knight in chain-mail, is pointed out to us, standing erect in a niche of the wall; and another singular feature is the small secret chamber within the tower, to which no sort of entrance has so far been discovered, while the only window has been built up, as appears in our view. History has little to say about Gillow, save that it was a seat of the powerful family of Pembruge, who settled here at least as early as the reign of Edward I.

GILLOW.

Our investigations at length completed, we pass out into the main road, and trudge the remaining distance into Ross, beneath the woods of Pengethley, and through little Peterstow, with its pleasant village green. As we proceed, the tall spire of Ross Church comes into sight, soaring high above the ruddy houses, which rise in steep terraces from the water's edge; and erelong we turn across Wilton Bridge, pausing beside a quaint old sundial to watch the graceful sweep of the stream beneath the massive arches, and to glance at the ivy-clad ruins of Wilton Castle, the mellow tones of whose crumbling stones are mirrored in the river beneath: and thence push on in the falling dusk of an early autumn evening through the streets of the bright little riverside town to the railway-station, in time to catch the last train to Hereford.

ALTERYNYS AND TREWYN.

AWAY in the extreme south-western corner of Herefordshire—where the dark waters of the Honddû, breaking from the circumjacent ranges of the Black Mountains, mingle their flood with that brisk little river the Monnow—lies a district which, in grandeur of scenery and variety of interest, is second to none in the county.

The great shoulders of Hatterel Hill, rising in bold and lofty cliffs from the vale of the Monnow, dominate the scene; and, by their marked contrast with the serrated peak of the Skyrrid and the dark-browed Sugarloaf Mountain, form a scene unrivalled in spacious dignity anywhere on this side the border.

The frequent recurrence of ancient camps and hill-stations, in conjunction with the traces of Roman roads through the district, suggest to the mind a condition of restless activity and oft-recurring *guerilla* warfare, between the ancient inhabitants of these mountain fastnesses, fighting for hearth and home, and the trained soldiers of the mighty Roman legions.

For many centuries this border-land must have been in an unsettled state; the castles at Longtown, Oldcastle, and elsewhere, being erected to control the wild march-men, and to bring the country into subjection under the Norman rulers. Many a wild and secluded spot is yet to be found in a day's ramble across the hills, where, in those long-past ages, the ancient Celtic inhabitants may well have found a haven of refuge from the ever-advancing tide of a superior civilization.

But enough now of ancient history: our committee of 'ways and means' ordains that we embark by a train leaving old Hereford at a convenient time in the morning; which, running past Pontrilas and giving us a passing peep at the ancient Court House, puts us down at Pandy Station in good time for a day's exploration of this fascinating district.

Shouldering our sketching-kit, we turn past the Pandy Inn, beloved of anglers, who find here a comfortable *pied à terre* after a day spent in beguiling the wary trout adown the charming reaches of the Monnow and her lively affluent, the Honddû.

Crossing a rustic bridge, a sharp turn on the right brings us to the farmhouse called Alterynys, which may be freely interpreted 'the island steep,' a name that, after the manner of Celtic place-names, graphically indicates its situation upon an abrupt neck of land almost encircled by the stream.

Despite its somewhat unpretending exterior, the house is interesting as having been, in early times, the home of the Cecil family, one branch of which is represented by our present prime minister, Lord Salisbury. Ancient Celtic writings record a certain Welsh knight named Robert Seisyllt, or Cecil, as engaged, about the latter half of the eleventh century, with the Norman Fitzhamon in the conquest of Glamorgan. Becoming enamoured of the Lady of Alterynys, he married and settled here, the family 'tree' at a later period including amidst its ramifications the name of Sir William Cecil, the great Lord Burleigh, that very sagacious statesman of good Queen Bess's golden days, whose grandfather, David Cyssell (who settled in Lincolnshire), was a descendant of Richard Cicele, sometime Forester of the royal manor of Ewias Harold.

In the fourteenth century the Grandisons dwelt at Alterynys, John Grandison, Bishop of Exeter, who died in 1369, being a native of this place. It is noteworthy that the families of Salisbury and Exeter derive their pedigree from the above-mentioned Robert Cecil of Alterynys. In the neighbouring church of Walterstone is preserved an ancient stained-glass window exhibiting the arms of Cecil, removed from Alterynys about a quarter of a century ago.

About the middle of the seventeenth century, Alterynys contained a great hall communicating with 'a faire Wainscott roome, usually emploied for a dining-roome,' which once could show handsome

ALTERYNYS.

armorial bearings of the Cecil family, emblazoned on the windows; here were also a gate-house and a green-court, in those times.

In the eighteenth century the Delahays possessed both this and the adjoining mansion of Trewyn; and are said to have planted the avenue of noble Scotch firs, which once extended across both estates.

The old house of Alterynys has been terribly ill-treated at the hands of later occupants; nevertheless, it still retains some traces of better days, notably a fine panelled ceiling, ornamented with the

Tudor rose and portcullis, and oak-leaves with acorns. Upstairs, a fine chamber with old oak wainscot is pointed out, in which Queen Elizabeth is said to have slept when on a visit to Sir William Cecil: at a corner of the landing a small door opens on a steep and narrow flight of old steps, which, upon investigation, prove to lead to a *cul-de-sac* amidst the open timbers of the roof; a weird, uncanny-looking spot, probably once used as a secret chamber.

Vestiges may be traced of extensive buildings, including a chapel, burnt down many years since, and some curious old ovens which, by their vast capacity, conveyed, we are told, a vivid impression of the scale upon which, in days of yore, the household was conducted.

We now turn our attention to the neighbouring mansion of Trewyn, whose steep gray roofs are discerned above the trees as we approach.

The original mansion, erected by the Harleys in the reign of Henry VII., was superseded by the present house, which was built, as is recorded by a date cut upon the stonework, in the year 1694; it is supposed to have been erected upon the site of an ancient tumulus, and is quite unlike any other mansion in this part of the country, having all the appearance of a French château, with its lofty windows, high-pitched roofs and broad flights of steps with intervening terraces, leading steeply up to the entrance-hall, each step being daintily adorned by a fringe of self-sown maidenhair-spleenwort, growing from the interstices of the stones.

In the twelfth century the manor of Trewyn was held by the Winstons, an ancient family who gave their name to the place, Tre-wyn signifying Wins-ton—the home of Win, or Gwyn. By the fifteenth century we find the estate passed to the Harleys, and subsequently the Delahays held Trewyn of the lords of Ewias Harold, and at the beginning of last century they were also in possession of Alterynys; at a later period the property passed by marriage to the Roshers, a family from Gravesend in Kent, whose descendant is the present owner of this interesting mansion.

Standing upon the broad terrace at Trewyn, a stately vista stretches before us, adown the long avenue of Scotch firs, whose salmon-tinted stems and broad masses of dark foliage still make a brave show, though bereft of many a tall comrade in a violent gale some years ago.

Close at hand, though hidden amidst dense foliage, is a pretty octagonal pigeon-house, erected in the olden times under the manorial right of dove-cot, near a field called the Chapel Meadow, where formerly stood an ancient chapel, long since demolished, dedicated to St. Martin. Evening and morning, at certain hours, the sound of the Angelus-bell is still heard across the vale; as in olden times when it served to guide the wayfarer to a resting-place here, on his journey across the mountains to Llanthony Priory.

By the courtesy of the kind *châtelaine,* we proceed to examine the beautiful panelled hall, with mantelpiece supported on huge pillars, brought from the ruined chapel of Alterynys; and the dining-room, whose walls are fitly adorned with relics of mediæval times. Here are preserved a battered Roman helmet, and a curious instrument called the 'branks,' a primitive appliance which was used to correct the vices of unruly 'scolds;' being placed over the head, with a gag between the teeth to curb the too-ready tongue. Here, too, are treasured a small silver arm and hand, portions of a statuette of the Venus Victrix, which has doubtless figured in many a triumphal procession of the Roman legions: we are also shown a finely illuminated old missal, which originally belonged to St. Mary's Abbey at Whitby.

Among other trophies which adorn the old walls are some fine heads of the otter; for this brave little animal yields lively pastime to the lovers of exciting sport, many being taken in the river Monnow, which here pursues a southerly course down a glen amidst wild scenery, in a channel whose 'crankling nookes' are well suited to the otter's love of seclusion.

In the grounds of Trewyn, traces of a Roman road—the 'Via Orientalis'—have been found, a portion of the great highway passing from Abergavenny to Kenchester, another part of which was exposed to view some years ago in the works of the Golden Valley Railway, near Abbey Dore; whence it passes, under the name of 'Stone Street,' in a direct line near Madley to the bend of the Wye at New Weir, where traces of the roadway and an ancient bridge have recently been brought to light.

Camps and moated mounds are scattered plentifully over this region, more particularly towards the Welsh border, where they were thrown up by the Saxon invaders to protect the lands wrested by them from the ancient owners of the soil. In the parish of Walterstone are some considerable remains of a British camp, which shows signs of having been occupied by the Romans, who enlarged it so as to serve for a protection to their road. Beyond Clodock, with its large parish church, stands Longtown Castle, once an important link in the chain of border fortresses; its circular keep-tower and ruined curtain-walls still bearing witness to the former strength of this abode of the Lacys.

To the visitor blessed with good walking powers, we can recommend a ramble over the hills which lie to the rear of Trewyn, whence it is five miles by open, moorland paths to Llanthony; with glorious widespread views, and a peep down into the secluded vale, with the dark mountains enfolding the ruined priory from the outer world, in a manner that is very striking. A vigorous climber may even compass the ascent of Pen Cader Vawr, whose dark summit frowns over the nearer shoulders of the ranges; but to do this a long day must be allowed, for scant is the accommodation for wayfarers in that wild region.

The wanderer among these hills cannot do better than take up his abode at the modest inn at Llanthony, once the prior's lodgings; where a room should be engaged beforehand, as visitors are numerous in summer time, and resting-places few and far between. Here the fisherman, artist or sportsman will find quiet, homely quarters; and a snug corner in the kitchen, where many a Rembrandtesque effect may be seen beneath the vaulted ceiling; while the country-side will provide matter to suit each individual taste.

Another delightful day may be spent by starting in good time from Pandy Station, and wandering across a broken and hilly country, climbing to the great camp of Twyn-y-Gaer, where we enter upon an outlying part of Herefordshire, whose strange, unpronounceable Welsh cognomen we will not attempt to inscribe. From this lofty hilltop the eye ranges across miles of wild, fern-clad mountain land, penetrated by the deep gorge of Cwm-Yoy, over which impends a beetling precipice, the scene of a vast landslip in some remote age.

We may now clamber down the steep western face of the hill, making in a 'bee-line' for a group of white cottages seen beyond the stream, which we cross by a rough tree-trunk and handrail, a simple apology for a bridge. The path going diagonally up the bank soon brings us to the unpretending little church at Patrisco, which, however, contains some remarkable features—to wit, an almost unrivalled rood-screen, with exquisite traceried front and carved frieze, now unhappily falling into disrepair; a very ancient font, with strange inscription in some antique character; and a primitively-conceived representation of Father Time (or perhaps of Death) with spade and hour-glass roughly drawn, fresco-wise, upon the western wall.

The return journey may be varied by taking a course down the valley, recrossing the stream by Pont-yspig, the Bishop's Bridge, so called from a local tradition that some prelate of olden times caused it to be built, in order that he might be enabled to visit these remote parishes: thence we push forward beneath the shadow of the massive Sugar-loaf Mountain, descending past the curious old farmhouse of Pen-y-clawdd, near which the double narcissus grows wild, to the railway-station at Llanvihangel Crucorney, by which imposing title this is identified among the four-and-twenty Llanvihangels to be found in Wales.

Waiting for the train, time is pleasantly spent in watching the changing effects of the last rays of sunset upon the rugged sides of the Skyrrid Mountain, which rises abruptly some two miles away. Now comes the up-train, bringing a momentary interval of bustle and hurry into the wayside station; and we are soon borne away past Pandy, whence we catch a last glimpse of the avenue at Trewyn, with lofty hills in the background; past Pontrilas and Kilpeck, and many another familiar haunt, till we find ourselves once more at our journey's end, amid the crowded streets of the time-honoured cathedral city.

BRANKS AT TREWYN.

ROUND ABOUT ROSS.

THERE is no scenery more characteristic of this Western shire than that of the district through which the river Wye meanders, in so vagrant a fashion, after breaking away from the city of Hereford; drawing her slow length along as though loath to quit this fair landscape, for the rapid and tortuous passage of her lower course to the Severn Sea.

Two routes are open to our choice—rail or river, rapid or romantic—whereby to extend our explorations into this favoured portion of the county. If time be no object, let the visitor by no means omit a cruise adown stream; but, for present purposes, we avail ourselves of the more speedy and convenient method of locomotion.

Running out of Barr's Court railway-station, we cross the Wye beneath the pretty villas of Hampton Park, and speed onwards beneath Dindor, or 'Oyster' Hill, beloved of picnic parties, which derives its singular name from the fact that Ostorius had a camp on the summit, vestiges of which may still be traced. Approaching a graceful sweep of the river, we pass within sight of the great mansion of Holme Lacy, one of the numerous estates granted by the Conqueror to his noble follower Walter de Lacy, and afterwards the home of the Scudamores, one of whom was, as we have seen, the restorer of the church of Abbey Dore. In the garden at Holme Lacy Rectory may be seen a singular pear-tree, of such a size as to form an orchard in itself, and yielding, it is said, fourteen to sixteen gallons of perry in a favourable season.

FAWLEY COURT
HEREFORDSHIRE

Henceforward we gain many a rapid glimpse of the sinuous Wye, now on this hand, now on that, as she

> 'To Ross her course directs, and right her name to showe ;
> Oft windeth in her waaie, as back she meant to go ;
> Meander, who is said so intricate to bee ;
> Hath not so many turnes, or crankling nookes as shee.'

Hanging woods, or broad level 'hams,' extend beside the placid reaches where, perchance, the salmon-fishers are plying their nets, or a cheery party of white-flannelled oarsmen are pulling easily down-stream.

Emerging from a short tunnel, we reach the next station, where we alight and walk across the open greensward to Fawley Court, a noble stone-built mansion, whose boldly-projecting mullioned windows yet retain a few remnants of stained glass; within, the spacious hall and handsomely-panelled rooms are probably little altered since this was the home of Sir John Kyrle, who died here in 1650 at the age of eighty-two.

Upon the peninsula formed by a bold sweep of the stream stands the little church at King's Caple, with its sharp steeple, perched atop of a hill; an ugly iron bridge leads us across the Wye to Hoarwithy, famous for its salmon-fishery and beautiful modern church, whose tall Italian campanile is a curious exotic amid this rural English scenery.

We now turn our backs for a time upon fair Vaga's stream, and strike inland past Llanfrother Farm—of which more anon—and through the clustering woods, where the sprightly rabbits stand, timid sentinels, with ears erect, adown the coppice sides; and a startled squirrel springs lightly away amidst the overarching branches.

Traces of ancient history linger in the names of 'Elverstone' and 'Athelstanes Woods,' recalling the far-away times of Queen Elfrida and the Saxon king, whose famous hunting is sung by the poet Mason, and depicted in a curious old painting preserved at Harewood House.

Harewood is a spacious stone structure of unmitigated Georgian type; more interesting to us is a well-restored chapel, originally built by the Knights Templars, containing monuments and stained-glass windows dedicated to members of the Hoskyns family, who for many generations were masters of Harewood. Here dwelt that remarkable man Sergeant Hoskyns, burgess of Hereford in the 'Addle Parliament;' who denounced King James for abuse of his prerogative, and who, for displaying 'too much wit and license,' was imprisoned in the Tower with Sir Walter Raleigh and Earl Percy of Northumberland. This Sergeant Hoskyns is reputed to have provided a novel entertainment for his sovereign, in the form of a morris-dance by five centenarian couples. His grandson was contemporary of John Evelyn, who remarks in his entertaining Diary: 'I was exceedingly importuned to stand the election; but desired their suffrages to be transferred to Sir John Hoskyns, a most learned virtuoso, as well as lawyer, who accordingly was elected.'

In traversing the finely-timbered park, where in spring-time the eye is greeted by

> 'A host of golden daffodils,
> Fluttering and dancing in the breeze,'

we diverge a few steps from the path to pay our respects to Harewood Oak, one of the largest trees in the county; a relic of the forest which once flourished here.

At the park gates we strike the Ross road, and bear away to the left past an inn where mine host owns the famous name of Scudamore. Close at hand, though hidden away in a hollow, is the moated house of Gillow, described in a previous chapter. We now turn over a stile near Pengethly, and, crossing a few fields, come suddenly upon the remote little church of Hentland, lying in a secluded nook, deep amidst woods and pastures. The ivy-clad tower looks down upon a quiet churchyard, adorned with an unusually perfect little Calvary cross, upon which may be traced a representation of the crucifixion, with figures standing below, and bearing, on the east and west faces, carved images of the Virgin and Child; the two corresponding sides showing the bishop and saint Dubricius, the patron saint of Hentland.

The great yew-tree which grows hard by is notable from the fact that its age is known; a record in the parish register showing that 'the Yew Tree between the Bell-house and the stile, was given by Philipe Swayne of Daviston: at the request of John Nourse, curate of

Hentland; and was removed and transplanted in the churchyard there, upon Shrove Tuesday; being the 13th day of February, Anno Dom. 1615.' A curious custom was observed at this church in olden times, when, upon Palm Sundays, cakes and ale were handed round to the parson and congregation; for which feast a neighbouring farm was laid under contribution.

At Llanfrother, of which we have already caught a glimpse, is the site of a college founded in the sixth century, respecting which Silas Taylor, in his 'History of Gavelkind,' says: 'In the region of Urchenfield, in a certain parish called Hên-Llan, commonly Hentland—which, in the English tongue, signifies "The Old Church"—and in certain pastures belonging to the church, there is a place which to this day is called Llanfrawtwr, which is as much as to say, "The Church or Convent of the Brethren," the site whereof was upon a small hill, not half a mile distant from Hentland; the ruins of which place, with its old foundations, are yet to be seen, and was a place dedicated to holy use; here it was that the great college for 100 students was founded by Saint Dubricius, the prince of this region (to repel the progress of the Pelagian Heresy); who succeeded his grandfather Pibanus, King of Ergin, the old name of Urchenfield, and in the days of King Arthur was made Archbishop of Caerleon.' This prelate officiated, in his capacity of Primate of the West British Church, at the coronation of King Arthur.

It is said that, at certain seasons, the foundation of large buildings may still be traced upon an eminence overlooking the Wye. In olden times this district, which comprehended that portion of Herefordshire lying south-west of the Wye, was governed by independent rulers; its ancient name survives to this day in the present ecclesiastical deanery of Archenfield.

Turning up a steep path beside the wood, a short mile brings us to 'Caradoc,' an Elizabethan mansion of noble proportions, situated on a lofty terrace overlooking a beautiful reach of the Wye; the spire of King's Caple, and the campanile tower at Hoarwithy showing prettily amidst a rich landscape.

'Caradoc' derives its name from the famous old British chieftain Caractacus, who is said to have lived here and ruled over this district.

The present stately dwelling-house is constructed mainly in the Elizabethan style; but, passing between the bright beds of a formal Italian garden, we gain access to the terrace, and thence obtain a view of an older, half-timbered portion of the house; whose quaint, uneven gables overlook the river, flowing far below.

Descending from 'Caradoc' by a crooked path down a leafy dingle, we descry, almost at our feet, the tall spire of Sellack Church; standing, with some half-dozen cottages, in a shady nook no great distance from the Wye. It is matter for marvel, what can have induced the founders to build their parish church in such an out-of-the-way spot as this, which, even in these latter days of highroads and railways, is by no means easy of access.

A somewhat singular appearance is produced by the curiously low tower, from which soars a disproportionately lofty spire; the large stone porch, quaint dormer window, sundial and churchyard cross—not to mention the curiously carved old tombstones—combine to form a highly picturesque exterior to this characteristic little country church: the interior, too, has an old-world, unrestored look about it; with oak pulpit and sounding-board, and side-chapel having a groined stone ceiling.

Traversing the waterside meadows, we strike the river in a few hundred yards; and, after a 'Yeo ho!' for the ferry, punt quietly across the full current, and so regain our path to Fawley Station, in time for the evening train, which speedily carries us to Ross; where we take up our quarters for the night at one of the comfortable hostelries with which this deservedly-favourite little town is well provided.

A stroll through the clean and well-kept streets reveals at every turn the name of John Kyrle, the 'Man of Ross' as he is fondly termed by the inhabitants, the 'bright particular star' of their firmament; who has been immortalized of late years by the philanthropic society whose kindly work is performed under the ægis of his name.

A turn past the market-place reveals Kyrle's fine old house, behind which lies a quaint garden and curious summer-arbour, with relics of the worthy man.

SELLACK.

John Kyrle was born in the neighbourhood, and spent his long life at Ross; where he gave many benefactions to the poor, and found employment for them in various occupations. He died in 1724, and was buried in Ross Church. Upon the occasion of the casting of one of the church-bells, which bears his name, Kyrle showed his loyalty by throwing his silver tankard into the furnace, after drinking to his king and country.

Hard by Kyrle's former abode, in the centre of the town, stands the market-house; built in the Italian style, during the reign of Charles II., probably upon the site of the ancient booth-hall. As a result of the wear and tear of two centuries, the pillars which support the fabric are reduced to grotesque forms, which adds to its picturesque appearance. On the gable is a panel containing a bust of Charles II., and upon the side-wall, over against John Kyrle's house, is a curious little 'logogram' which this loyal man caused to be carved upon the stonework, showing

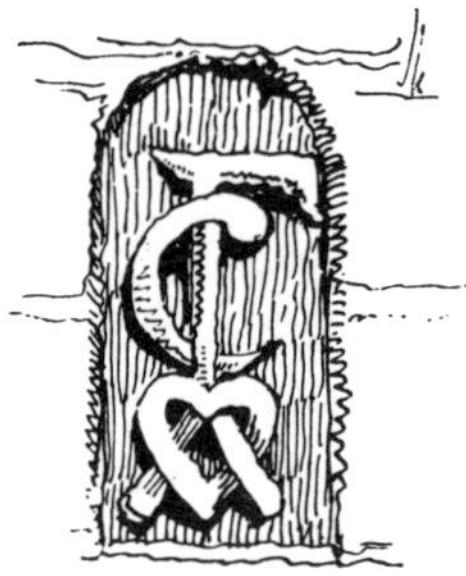

the letters F and C interlaced with a heart, which has been interpreted 'Faithful to Charles in Heart,' signifying the loyalty of Kyrle to the then newly restored monarch.

Passing on by the church, 'whose heaven-directed spire he taught to rise,' we enter the Prospect, a charming area of open greensward, with pleasant walks and benches, shaded by groups of noble elms planted by Kyrle. This popular resort commands a wide extent of fair landscape; through which the Wye sweeps in a noble horseshoe bend, beneath the broad terraces which rise towards the spectator.

MARKET-HOUSE, ROSS.

Resuming our stroll, some pretty 'bits' attract the eye, as we wander through the steep narrow streets; here, overlooking the churchyard, with its ancient pillar recording the time when Ross was stricken with the plague, stands the row of modest almshouses built by the Rudhalls, whose noble monuments in the church well repay a visit; there, rises a pretty gabled house-front, with latticed windows and balconies aglow with flowering plants and

OLD HOUSE AT ROSS.

creepers; such names, too, as Corpse-Cross Street and Edde-Cross Street, with De-la-Hays and Walwyns over the shop-fronts, suggest antiquarian associations.

From the upper end of the town we descend, by a steep road and flight of steps, to the point where town and river meet, at a spot still known as the Docks, whence boats may be hired for the Wye tour. In the Horseshoe Meadow, across the stream, we espy the remnants of a giant oak, estimated to be upwards of 300 years old. A curious circumstance in connection with this venerable tree is the fact that followers of 'the gentle art' may, in the days of good Queen Bess,

have sat on its branches and fished in the stream which now, owing to changes in the course of the river, flows at a furlong's distance across the broad meadow.

A pleasant walk, much favoured of Rossonians, leads beside the river to Wilton Bridge, usually a pretty lively scene, with country carts and market-folk; not to mention a handsome sprinkling of visitors bound to Goodrich or Wilton Castle, the ivy-clad ruins of the latter being observed hard by the bridge.

For many years after its erection, Wilton bridge was the only one across the Wye between Hereford and Monmouth; during the civil wars this was the scene of an engagement, in which Colonel Rudhall of Wilton Castle caused the arch on his side of the bridge to be destroyed, in order to arrest the advance of the Roundheads under Massey.

A few years previously, during the pestilential fever which occurred here in 1636, the inhabitants of Ross underwent a species of quarantine; when supplies for the ill-fated townsfolk were only allowed to enter by this route.

Wilton Bridge, with its massively constructed arches, boldly projecting cutwaters and quaint sundial, is built of the warm-coloured stone of the district, which, mellowed by the softening hand of time during some three centuries, forms a fascinating subject alike to artists and amateurs; some pretty peeps, too, are obtained from hereabouts of the old town of Ross, climbing steeply up the hill crowned by the tall church-spire, and reflected in the clear waters of 'devious Vaga.'

In the neighbourhood of Ross are two curious and interesting old mansions, known as 'Rudhall' and 'Wythall'—the Red and White halls *par excellence.* Rudhall is the growth of various periods; here Mr. Serjeant Rudhale built himself a residence, the grounds and offices covering, it is said, an area of eight acres.

One portion of the house was destroyed by fire in James I.'s time, beams of the original structure being yet traceable. Compartments of the hall-door bear the family motto, 'In Deo Confido'; and the bargeboards are elaborately carved. The red and white Tudor roses, the crown between two portcullises, and the plume of feathers enclosed in a garter, bearing the arms of Rudhall and Milborne at opposite ends, indicate the connection of the builder with Prince Arthur, son of Henry VII.

The name of Rudhall is considered by some to be a corruption of

WILTON BRIDGE.

Rood-hall; the mansion being locally supposed to stand at a point where four parishes unite, and near to an open space where once stood a cross, the meeting-place of those who, in olden times, engaged in 'beating the boundaries.'

The now extinct family of Rudhall were for many generations prominent in the district, and are represented by a fine group of table monuments in Ross Church. The recumbent figures of William Rudhall, serjeant-at-law of the time of Henry VII., and his wife, are very finely sculptured in Italian marble. John Rudhall, who died in 1636, is represented holding his wife by the hand; and close by, erect and—in the queer taste of that time—clad in the armour of a Roman general, stands William Rudhall, an officer of the Royalist army and the last male heir of this family.

Two miles from Ross, on the Walford road, stands Wythall, an unusually fine example of a timber mansion of the fifteenth century; it was erected by William Stratford, who held this estate about that period, and is one of the oldest mansions now existing in the county. John Stratford, at a more recent date, was a barrister of the Middle Temple and Recorder of Monmouth. He devised this property, after the death of his widow, to John Stratford Collins, the son of his nephew; the latter presided, when sheriff in 1744, at a memorable contest for the representation of the county, between the families of Cornewall, Foley and Harley.

The estate has continued in the Collins family down to the present time, being now held by Major John Stratford Collins.

Wythall remains little altered from its original condition; and, thanks to the interest shown by the family for their ancestral home, the house is stored with curious and interesting objects; here are preserved a fine carved and inlaid bedstead, bearing date 1621; oil-paintings by Sir Peter Lely; and an authentic portrait of Queen Elizabeth, given by her to a member of her court, which subsequently came into the possession of the Collins family.

The oak staircase is supported by a vast wooden pillar, which rises from cellar to roof, and is lighted by a lofty window of old stained glass of curious design; the windows of the upper rooms also, overlooking the quaint old garden at the rear, are of very unusual form, resembling the letter H; in honour, it has been suggested, of the reigning monarch, the mansion having been erected in the reign of Henry VI.

The parish of Walford, in which Wythall is situated, is held to have been the site of a Roman fortified station, to protect the adjoining ford across the Wye towards Goodrich; this must without question have been an important outpost, when the country beyond the river was still in the hands of the hardy natives of Siluria.

Following the main road past the fine old church at Walford, the tourist will make for Goodrich Castle, whose rugged bastions may be seen, embowered amidst trees, upon an eminence rising abruptly from the river which washes the base of the cliff. Carriage-folk must needs follow the road which crosses the Wye at Kerne Bridge; but the pedestrian has the alternative of a delightful approach to the castle, by taking the lane to the right at Walford Church, and striking across the meadows to a ferry; hence the ruins are seen to great advantage, crowning the bold promontory, around which the river sweeps in a broad reach beneath hanging woods, a group of white-faced cattle standing, perchance, knee-deep in the clear water.

It was while crossing at this ferry that Henry IV., then Earl of Derby, first heard of the birth of his son, afterwards Harry of Monmouth. In honour of the event, the earl forthwith presented to the boatman the ferry and all perquisites therefrom, and the descendants of this fortunate ferryman continued in enjoyment of the gift for several centuries.

The river crossed, we ascend a steep path which affords some pretty views of the wooded slopes overtopped by the battlements of Goodrich Court, a noble castellated mansion, where the celebrated Meyrick collection of armour was formerly deposited.

After a further climb, we enter the castle ruins through the breach made by the guns of Cromwell's forces, and, passing under the 'Ladye's Tower,' with its lofty pillar supporting two graceful arches, gain the courtyard; where we are greeted by an elderly dame, who assures

RUDHALL.

us that she well recollects the poet Wordsworth conversing with her, when a child, at the castle, and who claims to have been the identical little maiden immortalized in 'We are Seven.'

At the extreme end of the courtyard rises the Anglo-Saxon keep-tower, the most ancient part of the castle, whose massive gray walls are pierced by round-arched windows overlooking the court; the side

GOODRICH CASTLE.

facing the open country in the rear being built without openings, to insure safety against attacks from that quarter. This is sometimes called Macbeth's Tower, from a tradition that it was built by an Irish chieftain of that name, as a ransom for himself and his sons. To the left stands another tower, containing the state prison, with curious devices incised upon the inner walls. On the right of the keep rises the Great Tower, a vast circular structure with peculiar buttresses, which figures in many a sketch of the ruins. Adjoining the latter are the remains of the banqueting-hall, overlooking the pleasaunce, and connected with the Ladye's Tower. This side of the courtyard, it may be observed, was occupied by the state apartments of the 'lord's habitation,' the opposite or southern side containing the quarters of the garrison and men-at-arms, and the great Gateway, the most complete portion of the buildings; the latter still retains grooves for the triplet of portcullises, and rows of machicolations for pouring down molten lead, to afford a warm reception to an enemy. In the long passage beyond the drawbridge may be noticed the loophole through which messages were delivered to the guard, ere the gates were opened to admit the visitor. Alongside the gateway stands the Chapel, retaining some details of stone carving and tracery; beyond this rises the Beacon-tower, which figures prominently in our sketch.

Surrounding the castle extends a deep and wide moat, hewn out of the solid sandstone rock, of which the ruins are constructed; which, in the lapse of time, has assumed lovely tints of varying reds and grays, relieved by splashes of brilliant bronze and golden-hued lichens. Around and within the moat, a luxuriant growth of trees and shrubs veils the old walls in a mantle of delicate green foliage; while the ruined bastions which once frowned upon the drawbridge are now wreathed in masses of dark ivy.

Although there is no doubt that a stronghold has existed here from very ancient times, the earliest authentic record concerning it is of the date of 1204; at which time Goodrich Castle was given by King John to William Strigul, earl-marshal, to hold by the service of two knights' fees. At a subsequent period Goodrich passed to the noble family of Talbot; one of whom, Richard by name, expended large sums, obtained from the ransoms of his French prisoners, in improving the castle.

Richard's descendant, John Talbot, the great Earl of Shrewsbury, who was buried at Rouen during the wars with France, was sub-

WYTHALL.

sequently reinterred at Whitchurch in Shropshire, where his remains were recently discovered; the title of 'Lord of Goderich and Orchenfield' appearing upon his monument.

Goodrich Castle afterwards came to Henry de Gray, Earl of Kent, by his marriage with Elizabeth, daughter and heiress of Lord Gilbert Talbot; and the estates continued in the possession of this family until A.D. 1740, when they were purchased by the family of Admiral Griffin, of Hadnock, Monmouthshire.

During the civil wars this important fortress was alternately held by the Royalist and the Parliamentary forces; but eventually, in 1646, a party of the king's troops, under Sir Richard Lingen, withstood a prolonged siege by the famous Colonel Birch, of which some curious details were given by the 'war correspondents' of the period, in the *Perfect Diurnal* and other contemporary journals.

From the castle we find a footpath leading to the village of Goodrich, passing near a quaint little structure known as 'Y Crwys,' presumably from its position at the cross-roads, where the lane runs down to the ferry. A short distance away in the direction of the railway-station lie the picturesque ruins of Flanesford Priory, founded A.D. 1347 by Richard Talbot for canons of St. Augustine, but now used as a barn.

Crossing a stile, we enter a field-path which, winding up a steep bank, brings us to the church, whose tall spire is a conspicuous object in the landscape. For several centuries the Swift family, ancestors of the famous dean, were connected with Goodrich, his grandfather being ejected from the living by the king's opponents, for a too fervent display of loyalty. Here is preserved an elegant silver communion-cup, presented to the church, as an inscription records, by the Rev. Jonathan Swift, in the year 1726.

In the churchyard we notice a curious monument erected to a clergyman named Herbert, in the form of a gigantic block of conglomerate stone, some twelve feet long, which was dragged from the foot of Doward Hill, and placed here according to the known wishes of the deceased man, a traction-engine being required for the purpose, which necessitated the taking down of a portion of the churchyard wall.

Turning past the vicarage garden, we enter the Monmouth road, which leads beneath the ridge of Copped Wood Hill, and approaches a bend of the river. A mile further we pass through Whitchurch, a picturesque village beneath the steep side of Doward Hill, whose rocky ribs are honeycombed by the caverns known as 'King Arthur's Halls.'

Time will not permit us to climb to the British Camp which crowns the summit, so we turn sharp to the left and pursue the by-road which 'hugs' the river bank. Steep, wooded hills close around us as we advance—outliers of the adjacent Forest of Dean, within whose leafy glades nestle quaint old mining villages, where, time out of mind, the good people have followed the same calling as in the days when the Romans first explored the rich coal measures, which spread away hence to the shores of the distant Severn Sea.

Our shadows lengthen before us as we descend to the ferry at Symonds Yat, and in floating across the full current we catch a charming glimpse of this beautiful spot, for

'The moon is up, and yet it is not night,'

—the glow of the setting sun still lingering upon the higher summits, whose warm tints are repeated in the clear stream beneath, which is fretted with golden splashes from the lights at the water-side. A white mist rising, softly veils the precipitous sides of the gorge; whence the giant rock-pinnacles of the 'Seven Sisters' stand boldly out from amidst the tangle of wild undergrowth at their feet.

Here, at length, we come to an end of our wanderings amidst the romantic and beautiful scenery, for which this rural English county is so justly admired; where it has been our good fortune to experience an old-world courtesy from the dwellers in these 'haunts of ancient peace' —be it in cottage or time-worn grange—that causes pleasant memories to linger of many a kindly welcome to the wayfarer rambling, sketch-book in hand, amid the 'Nooks and Corners of Herefordshire.'

JOHN KYRLE'S TANKARD.

INDEX.

26

Elliot Stock, 62, Paternoster Row, London.

LIST OF SUBSCRIBERS.

Adnitt, H. W., Shrewsbury.
Alcock, Miss, Hyde.
Allen, Mrs., Ross, Herefordshire.
Army and Navy Stores, Victoria Street, S.W.
Atlay, Miss, The Palace, Hereford.
Attwood-Mathews, B. St. John, Pontrilas Court, Herefordshire.
Aveline, G. E., Chalford, Gloucestershire.
Aymard, A. A., Somerset House.

Banks, W. H., Ridgebourne, Kington.
Barneby, W. Henry, Bromyard.
Bartleet, Rev. S. E., Gloucester.
Barton, T., Lancaster.
Baskerville, Mrs., Canon-ffrome Court, Ledbury.
Bateman, Right Hon. Lord, Shobdon.
Beaufort, Rev. D. A., Lewisham.
Bellamy, C. H., Manchester.
Bellers, Lieut.-Colonel R. B., Worcester.
Black, Rev. C., M.A., Colwall, Malvern.
Blacklock and Son, Leominster.
Blackwell, B. H., Oxford.
Brodribb, Rev. W. Kennedy, Ledbury.
Buckle, Rev. J., M.A., Ashperton, Ledbury.
Bulkeley-Owen, Rev. T. M., Oswestry.
Bulwer, General, Norfolk.
Burd, Rev. Prebendary, Shropshire.

Caddick, E., Edgbaston.
Carless, J., Jun., St. John Street, Hereford.
Carter, Eric M., N. Bromsgrove.
Carter, Mrs. E., Cheltenham.
Cave, E. L., Bromyard.
Chapman, H. M., Canterbury.
Clements, H. J. B., Celbridge, Ireland.
Cobbold, Rev. Prebendary R. H., The Rectory, Ross.
Colt, E. W., M.A., Rugeley, Staffs.
Conder, Edward, Colwell, Herefordshire.
Consterdine, J. P., Kingstone, Herefordshire.
Cornewall, Rev. Sir. G. H., Bart., Hereford.
Cornish Bros., Birmingham (3 copies).
Cresswell, G., Hereford.
Culshaw, Rev. G. H., M.A., Hereford.

Davies, J., Hereford.
Davies, James, Gwyfna, Brooney Hill, Hereford.
Davies-Burlton, T., Eaton Hill, Leominster.
Deakin, S., Edgbaston.
Downing, Wm., Birmingham.

Ebrall, S., Shrewsbury.
Eckersley, J., Adlington.
Elkington, G., Edgbaston.
Ely, Mrs., Handsworth.

Farrah, J., Low Harrogate.
Fellows, A., Harborne.
Firmstone, Rev. E. R., Herefordshire.
Fisher, E., Newton Abbot.
Fisher, S. T., Streatham.
Foley, P., Prestwood, Stourbridge.
Forbes, E., Bromyard.
Free Library, Hereford.

Gillespie, General, Abergavenny.
Gray, Henry, Leicester Square, W.C.
Griffiths, Richard, Newcourt, Hereford.
Guest, W. H., Manchester.
Guildhall Library, London, E.C.

Hampden, Mrs., London, S.W.
Hanbury, Mrs., Hereford.
Hanbury, Rev. T., Church Langton Rectory.
Harford, F., Beckenham.
Harrold, Miss C., Edgbaston.
Haslam, Wm. F., Edgbaston.
Haslewood, Rev. F. G., Canterbury.
Hebb, Wm., Herefordshire.
Hemnan, W., Edgbaston.
Henderson, D. G., West Dulwich.
Heywood, J., Manchester.
Hibbert, Miss Ellen, Birkenhead.
Higgins, Mrs., Thing-Hill, Hereford (3 copies).
Hopton, Rev. M., B.A., Canon Frome Vicarage, Ledbury.
Humfrys, W. J., Hereford.
Hutchinson, A., Hagley Park, Hereford.

Jakeman and Carver, Hereford.
Jeffcoatt, T., Queen's Gate, S.W.
Jenkins, Mrs., Holmer, Hereford.
Jones, Miss, Richmond Place, Hereford.

Keene, R., Derby.
King, W. W., Stourbridge.
Knowles, Rev. C., Winteringham Rectory.

Layton, C. Miller, Folkestone.
Lingen, Right Hon. Lord, Wetherby Gardens, London, S.W.
Llanwarne, T., Norfolk House, Hereford.
Lloyd, E. P., Leominster.
Lloyd, J. H., Highgate.
Lloyd, J. W., Kington.
Lutwyche, H. Latham, Kyneston, Ross.

Mayo, Rev. T., Bridgnorth.
McKibbin, J., Dresden, Saxony.
McLaughlin, Rev. A. H., Newark.
Meynell, His Honour Judge, Durham.
Mills, R. E., St. James's Street, S.W.
Mitchell, F. J., Newport, Mon.
Moore, H. C., Broad Street, Hereford.
Morgan, Rev. H. G., Stoke Lacy Rectory, Bromyard.
Muntz, Mrs., Umberslade.
Murray, Oscar, Bedford.
Musgrave, John, Whitehaven.
Mynors, Rev. W. B., Llanwarne Rectory, Herefordshire.

Nicholls, Judge, Benares, India.
Nixon, E., Leeds.

Oldham, Captain C. D., Hereford.

Paley, E. G., Lancaster.
Palin, Rev. E., Linton, Ross.
Pashley, R., Rotherham.
Payton, G. H., Edgbaston.
Permanent Library, Hereford.
Phelps, General, Edgbaston.
Phillips, Moro, Chichester.
Phillott, G. H., Cheltenham.
Phillott, Rev. Chancellor, Hereford.
Pilley, J. B., Hereford.
Piper, G. H., Ledbury.
Powell, Rev. F., Hereford.
Prescott-Decie, Colonel Richard, Tenbury.
Pritchard, C., Edgware, Middlesex.
Putman, Mrs. M. Lowell, Boston, U.S.A.

Ramsey, R., Glasgow.
Randall, J., Sheffield.
Reece, Mrs., Edgbaston.
Reynall, Father, Belmont Pro-Cathedral, Hereford.
Reyner, Mrs. J. B., Ashton-under-Lyne.
Ridgway, E., Liverpool.
Rigby, R., Stoke-on-Trent.
Roberts, C. M. Compton, Drybridge, Monmouthshire.
Rootes, C., Hereford.
Rusby, Rev. W. H. Lees, Worcester.

Sibbald, J. G., Admiralty.
Simpson, E. K., Ipswich.
Skinner, Wm., Edinburgh.
Smith, R. G., Hull.
Smith, Thomas, A.C.A., Hereford.
Smith, W. A., Birmingham.
Sotheran, H., and Co., Strand, W.C.
Southall, H., Ross, Hereford.
Sparrow, A., Shrewsbury.

Stanhope, Hon. and Ven. Archdeacon Hereford.
St. Aubyn, J. P., Cornwall.
Steavenson, A. L., Durham.
Stephens, E., Hereford.
St. John, Rev. H. F., Dinmore Manor, Herefordshire.
Stokes, D. G., Chippenham.
Stokes, Miss, Hereford.
Studholme, P., Parsonstown.
Sturges, Rev. H. C., M.A., Leominster.
Swainson, Rev. J. G., Wistanstow Rectory.
Swinburne, Mrs. W. A., Dulas Hay, R.S.O.

The Rev. the Warden St. Michael's College, Tenbury.
Thompson, J., Wilmslow.
Thornhill, E. B., Primrose Hill Road.
Thornhill, Miss.
Tilley, Luke, Ledbury.
Timmins, F. H., Edgbaston.
Timmins, Mrs., Edgbaston (3 copies).
Tomkins, Rev. H. G., Weston-super-Mare.
Trafford, H. R., Michaelchurch Court, Hereford.
Tregear, Mrs. Cardine, India.
Turner, W. H., Maidstone.

Underwood, E. M., Castle Street, Hereford.

Vaughan, J. W., Radnorshire.
Vincent, Wm., Norwich.

Waldo Sibthorp, H. A. M., Chester Square.
Walker, W., Finsbury Park.
Ward, H., Stafford.
Watkins Bros., Hereford.
Wellard, C., Bromley-by-Bow, E.
Weyman, Henry, Ludlow, Salop.
Whitaker-Bean, J., London.
Whitefoord, Rev. P., Tenbury.
Whitwell, Henry, Edgbaston.
Willett, Henry, Brighton.
Williams, H. R., Hornsey.
Willis, J., Birmingham.
Wilson, C. M., Sheffield.
Winter, Mrs., Bodenham Road, Hereford.
Woodhouse, Miss E., Burghill Court, Herefordshire.
Wood, J. B., Ludlow.
Wood, J. H., Ledbury.
Wood, Mrs. S. F.

LARGE PAPER COPIES.

Arkwright, J. H., Hampton Court, Leominster.
Beddoe, H. C., Castle Street, Hereford.
Brimmer, Mrs. Martin, Boston, U.S.A.
Caddick, E., Edgbaston.
Clarke, T. Ward, Hereford.
Denny, Messrs., Strand, W.C.
Foley, P., Prestwood, Stourbridge.
Free Library, Hereford.
Gibson, Denston, Edgbaston.
Gray, Henry, Leicester Square, W.C.
Hill, Thomas Rowley, St. Catherine's Hill, Worcester.
James, F., Cromwell Road, S.W.
Parry, J. H., Herefordshire.
Pateshall, Mrs., Allensmore Court, Herefordshire.
Perkins, Mrs. A. T., Boston, U.S.A.
Pilley, W., Hereford.
Vassar-Smith, R. V., Cheltenham.